UFO WARNING

John Stuart

SAUCERIAN PUBLISHER

ISBN:978-1-955087-26-1

PROLOGUE

It is generally a good idea to return to the classics in any genre. This also goes for UFO literature. Rereading a book, or reviewing old documents after ten or twenty years is a rewarding experience. You will discover new data and ideas you didn´t notice before. The reason, of course, is that you are, in many ways, not the same person reading the book the second or third time. Hopefully you have advanced in knowledge, experience, intellectual and spiritual discernment. A good starting point is to reread the contactee classics material of the 1960s, in order to understand the deeper mystery involved in what happened during that era.

John Stuart's strange story appeared in *UFO Warning* 1963), published by Gray Barker's Saucerian Books for the first time in the early 60's. In his introduction to *UFO Warning*, Gray Barker said:" I cannot completely understand this volume, and I don't think that many others can either…In its rawest and most immediate sense, it will serve as a warning to many UFO students!"

John Stuart began in 1950 by collecting UFO clippings from around the world and reading all books that he could on the subject. One evening around 1952, Stuart received a knock at his door, and nobody was there when he went out. Stuart suspected that this incident was not a mere kid fulling around and somehow related to his flying saucer investigations. Not long after this incident, Stuart was in bed reading late one night when his telephone rang, and on the other end was an anonymous caller (from another planet who warned him to "Stop interfering in affairs that don't concern you! You have been warned!" This warning was not enough for Stuart, and in 1953 he joined a UFO research group based out of Hamilton, New Zealand, called the Flying Saucer Investigation Society. After a few months with the group, Stuart fell in love with another group member and left to found his organization, Flying Saucer Investigators (FSI). Joining Stuart in this endeavor was this "group member" named Doreen Wilkinson (named in *UFO Warning* as Barbara Turner.) The only two members of Stuart's group were Stuart himself and Wilkinson. Gene Duplantier's cover for UFO Warning has nothing to do with the story that appeared in this book. It seems that Duplantier was the forerunner of the Ancient Alien Theorists. This book is a facsimile reproduction of the original printed text in shades of gray. Because this material is culturally important, we have made it available as part of our commitment to protect, preserve and promote knowledge in the world. This book has been formatted from its original version for publication. **IMPORTANT, although we have attempted to maintain the integrity of the issues accurately, the present reproduction could have missing and blurred pages and poor pictures due to the age of the original scanned copy.** Because this material is culturally important, we have made it available as part of our commitment to protect, preserve and promote knowledge in the world. This book was one of the first to describe the aliens as threat.

Editor
Saucerian Publisher. 2022

UFO WARNING

By JOHN STUART

UFO WARNING

By JOHN STUART

I would like to record my sincere gratitude to Gray Barker for the assistance he gave me during the period Flying Saucer Investigators operated. In the New Zealand idiom, Gray was always, and still is, a "fair dinkum cobber." He stuck by me as a sincere friend when my own countrymen who were investigators and researchers deserted me, refusing to accept my word that I had known some strange experiences.

Never once did he question my word, nor refused to accept my data without having the absolute physical proof which I could not give him.

If, in the publication and the printing of my manuscript, Gray sticks out his neck out too far and gets it chopped off, I shall be truly sorry -- but not dismayed. For, as he has been capable of doing in the past, he will only grow a longer one.

John Stuart
Hamilton, New Zealand
1963

INTRODUCTION

Most readers of this volume will have known of John Stuart through the reading of my own book, "They Knew Too Much About Flying Saucers (University Books, 1956).

He was one of the researchers, which I told about, who had been "hushed," (using popular Ufological terminology) after finding out what was perhaps too much about Flying Saucers. In my book I recorded the explanation that John furnished me at that time.

As this volume will develop, I was unable to present the actual facts of the matter as John now writes them, because he felt it necessary at that time to mislead me a little so that his information had some chance of being believed.

In this respect he acted no differently than did Albert K. Bender, who, in his recent volume, "Flying Saucers and the Three Men," honestly admits that he misled many people in order to protect himself.

I believe that anybody who reads this volume by Stuart and Bender's book will instantly forgive these researchers for a bit of deception which they felt was tremendously important while they were in danger.

What you are about to read is, to me, a far more shocking account than you read in Al Bender's book. It is a book which is unpleasant for me to publish. It is a book which is unpleasant for you to read.

But it is a book which neither I the publisher, nor you the reader, can overlook. Nor censor. Nor hide somewhere with the hope that nobody will read it and be warned by it.

John Stuart's unpleasant experiences were not presented to you in this form until after we had given the matter of its publication a great deal of thought. I think that the decision to publish it came from the innate and irrepressable instincts of a reporter rather from the sound judgment of a commercial publisher.

Although I cannot completely understand this volume, and I doubt if many others can either, it is a definite part of the huge mass of confusing data which has so far formed the UFO enigma. It may be helpful to others, who possess a greater understanding than do I, and assist them in uncovering hidden facets of the Flying Saucer Mystery. In its rawest and most primary sense it will serve as a warning to many UFO students, since it will inform them that within the framework of the Enigma exists pitfalls which can cause grief and danger. I would not want this book to construe, however, the idea that everybody should give up UFO research because there are evidently certain negative areas involved, which can be tapped and unleashed, causing great pain.

Those who are as familiar as am I with the field of flying saucers know decisively of the frustrating inability we have experienced in obtaining and offering incontravertable physical proof of the existence of such objects. This we have tried to do, without a complete understanding of why we have tried it. So far I think we can be highly satisfied, however, with the by-products of this frustrating quest.

To a materialist, which I represent, such by-products are not hard to demonstrate in a physical sense. Higher than the possibility of life on other worlds, physical and spiritual assistance from space people, I value the friends I know, personally, and by correspondence, whom I have gained through the pursuit of this subject.

Other people, I am quite certain, can look deeper into these by-products, and find non-material values which may likewise transcend actual proof or solution to the mystery.

What I have gained, I do know, has been of a positive nature. In the logical expression of a universe, however, there must exist, also, negative influences. This volume, most capably, expresses such. As a part of the definitive literature on this subject, this work also becomes a responsibility, literarily speaking.

Its interpretation will also be varied and hotly argued. Perhaps some sort of a definite conclusion can be reached after it is widely read and discussed -- yet I doubt it.

An understanding of negative influences cannot be gained

from the sidelines. They must be met, experienced, fought and repelled before such understanding comes. These influences can take many forms: unpleasant and lecherous monsters, in the case of John Stuart; three frightening men in the case of Bender; in our own case misfortunes and harrassments of various sorts.

If the struggle with Satan were easy, the muscles of the Angels would be flabby. If the Bad were not tragic and unpleasant, the paths of Heaven might be lesser trod.

The book you are about to read will be discussed by psychologists, rehashed by demonologists, burned by cowards, and alternately be used as ammunition by and preached against by Preachers.

I personally don't know quite what to think of it; but I know that I must publish it.

What do you think?

Gray Barker
1963

CONTENTS

GLOSSARY 13

ONE: THE BEGINNING 15

TWO: MY FIRST WARNING 18

THREE: SAUCERS AN "INSIDE JOB"? 20

FOUR: THE THING IN THE DESERT 22

FIVE: THE UFO MAP 25

SIX: ANCIENT PEOPLES AND THE UFO 29

SEVEN: R.A.F. REPORTS OBJECT 35

EIGHT: BARBARA'S STRANGE ACTIONS 41

NINE: THE PEOPLE OF THE POLES 46

TEN: THE VISITOR 51

ELEVEN: THE SECRET OF THE SPHINX 55

TWELVE: I SEE THE DISC 60

THIRTEEN: THE HIDEOUS THING 64

FOURTEEN: THE CREATURE RETURNS 71

FIFTEEN: THE ENDING 77

GLOSSARY

Certain New Zealand slang terms appear in this book, and are translated here to their real meanings in English.

"FAIR DINKUM" : Genuine. Real. Serious.

"DICKEN" : Wait on. Just a minute.

"STREWTH" : An abbreviation for the words, "God's Truth."

"STRIKE!" : A term used by soldiers in the First World War, being in full, "Strike a light!" Also meaning, generally, an exclamation such as "Gosh!" or "Gee!"

"COBBER" : This term is used only in Australia and New Zealand, and means, "Friend."

"SHE'S RIGHT!" : Used ONLY in New Zealand. Means "That's all right."

"CRIKEY" : This is a derivative of the word, "Christ," and is sometimes spoken as "Cripes," although the latter is more peculiar to Australia.

"STOUSH" : A Kiwi soldier's term for "Fight," or "Battle."

"RIGHT-OH" : Another way of saying "Allright," and used on both sides of the Tasman Sea, in Australia and New Zealand.

CHAPTER ONE
THE BEGINNING

I began an active study of the UFO Enigma in 1948 and, over the first few months, dealt only with the few reports available. They came mainly from America, with one or two from Australia. My first belief was that these strange objects were interplanetary space vehicles.

At that time one could suggest little else -- for the idea that Antarctica was involved did not occur to anyone connected with the investigation. In fact, it was not until 1953 that such an idea was born in my own mind. Once I accepted it as fact, the "uncanny" began with shocking results for my co-worker and myself.

It was during 1950 that I decided to form my own society; this was planned to bring together those New Zealanders interested in this new mystery, and to attempt what appeared to be the impossible: find the answer as to what the UFOs were, and from where they originated. I also wished to know why they were coming to Earth's skies, and why they had not landed to make known their intentions.

I made a note at that time, referring to the fact that the UFOs might be interested in man's devilish new toy, the Atom Bomb, and its effect on Earth-dwellers. I also noted: "Interest in man may be clinical? Why?" This note, I see today, was filled with tremendous questions, each of which concluded with one word: "WHY?" It was a challenge, and I accepted it. I was determined to pit my own wits against those of people (?) who controlled these discs.

But what could a mere 28-year-old Kiwi do to learn this secret? There was only one way. I would have to use my own common sense and work on a process of elimination. And then I had to decide how one began to investigate a mystery such as this. The only evidence we had was the fact that a few "strange disc shaped craft were sighted over (say) Washington." Why? What had they hoped to find? What were they searching for? What made them "tick"? Who owned them? Of questions I had an enormous number, but the facts were not yet at hand. I was determined to search out those facts. It was a challenge to a young New Zealander. I accepted it, and planned the formation of my own society, but the results of a war wound, a legacy of El Alamein, stopped my ideas for some time.

In 1952 I contacted Harold H. Fulton, who had founded Civilian Saucer Investigation, of Auckland, New Zealand, and kept him up to date on reports from my own city and immediate area. Later, through wide correspondence, I received reports from all over the world, and also passed this along to Fulton. At first it was a most amicable association, but later it developed into something far removed from a friendship. I was urged on in my dedicated quest for information, and in my quiet research I contacted as many fellow researchers as I could in other countries, offering whatever assistance I could give. Many such researchers did not accept my offers to help, but those who did remained with me -- the most of them almost to the end. One of them stuck with me even through that.

The Hamilton, N. Z., Flying Saucer Investigation Society was formed in April, 1953, and I was appointed Secretary. At the initial meeting I told those present of the five UFOs I had sighted in the preceeding seven years, the first being in November, 1946, the second in 1947, the third in the same year. The next was on Easter, 1953; and two nights later I experienced another sighting, that one witnessed by my wife.

My association with the Hamilton organization lasted only about six months, after which I was expelled in "disgrace." I had worked out a theory about UFOs and had inadvertantly used a copy of the Society's letterhead. The Committee objected to this, and I was expelled from their very august gathering, being allowed no chance to defend my action, since I was not informed of the meeting.

As a result of this expulsion by H.F.S.I.S., I suggested to a young lady friend that we immediately form our own organization to attack the mystery along the lines of the theory I had developed. She enthusiastically agreed, and it was from this suggestion that Flying Saucer Investigators (the formal name of our organization) was born.

We carried on this research until December, 1954, when we were forced to close down after very frightening attacks from an unknown source. In that month Barbara fled in terror, and I went to Auckland to recover my normal health with my old mother. My trip to Auckland was much different from the evil-minded suggestions that I had "gone away with that girl"!

Two and a half years later I returned to my home with the intentions of carrying out further research, but again I closed the organization, thinking of the real theory I had regarding the UFOs. Also, I remembered the dissolute and nefarious things which were said when I escorted Barbara to the cinema, or when we strolled in the moonlight, talking of our views and findings about UFOs. These cinema visits and walks were quite innocent, but the depraved minds of those who secretly watched saw only the suggestion of sensuality, the only thing their insidious minds were capable of seeing.

And so, while these evil minds concocted filthy thoughts of Barbara and me, we carried on in our attempts to solve the mystery, our time being fully taken up with our task. It is admitted that we did find time to "act the goat," and at these times I have kissed my co-worker, a fact which was pointed out to me by one of the busy-bodies. I wonder still wherein lies the sin of kissing a girl in friendship or in jest!

CHAPTER TWO
MY FIRST WARNING

During my research I encountered many experiences which I could only construe as being frightening, or, at the least, strange. It is difficult for me to determine if all of these experiences were connected with my UFO research, or to determine which were and which weren't. The first such experience, which I now relate, probably should be listed under the "weren't" heading, but it is definitely a part of my narrative. The date escapes me, but it happened in 1951 or 1952, as I was standing in the lounge doorway, smoking a cigarette.

The house was quiet, and I was thinking of ordinary matters, as I faced the front door, about five feet away. Suddenly I heard footsteps on the concrete path outside, and I wondered who might be calling at such a late hour. The doorbell rang and I stepped forward to greet my visitor.

No more than two or three seconds passed from the time the bell rang until I had the door open, and I was surprised and puzzled to find nobody there! I ran outside, hoping to catch the prankster. I searched the grounds without result. I was indeed puzzled, for whoever had rung my doorbell would not have had time to escape without my observing or hearing them running away. I wondered if there were indeed such things as ghosts, though I found the thought amusing and chuckled. Later, when I informed Barbara of the incident, she immediately suggested it might have involved something of supernatural nature. I laughed at her and told her I thought those things were just so much rot. Later, though, I remembered those words!

The doorbell incident first returned to mind some time in 1952, at about 11:30 P.M. I was in bed, reading, when my telephone rang. I was a trifle annoyed as I picked up the phone to answer such a late call, then even more annoyed as the following conversation took place:

"Are you John Stuart?"

"That is correct."

"You are the John Stuart who is interested in what earth men call flying saucers?"

"That's right. What can I do for you?"

"I warn you to stop interfering in affairs which do not concern you!"

"Who the hell are you talking to, mate? And who the flaming hell are you!"

"I am ???????????? from another planet." (The name I cannot remember because it seemed to be unpronounceable)

"Go to hell!" (Again I was warned, the voice adding the dangers I would face if I failed to take heed)

"Beware, Earthman!"

"You and who else, mate?" (This will serve as my answer, for the actual words I used I would not want to appear in this book)

"You have been warned!"

The line suddenly went dead.

As I slowly replaced the receiver, my mind was alert to the words I had just heard. My first reaction was to treat it as a hoax, but when I sat down with a pot of beer I began to wonder.

The voice had been most strange. In quality it was like a machine talking to me -- expressionless, cold. But that cold tone only added to its meaning. I shuddered and drank my beer. The warning had been given. Why? What did I know that was so important to this person -- or thing? What did I know which was more revealing than, say, what Fulton had learned?

I lit a cigarette and told myself that some half-baked drongo had been playing games with me. I nodded. That was the answer. The world was full of these simple-minded people who had nothing better to do than play games which even a child would scorn.

CHAPTER THREE
SAUCERS AN "INSIDE JOB"?

Reflecting further on the telephone call, I was forced to consider the possibility that it MIGHT have been genuine. What then? But whether it had been a hoax or the real thing, I knew that I must ignore the threat. I had fought in a war for my freedom, and I wasn't going to be pushed around! Why, I mentally demanded, should some unknown person or thing tell me what to do? Again I told them to "go to hell and do your worst" in my thoughts. Later I was to believe the owner of the voice had heard those thoughts -- for "they" did do their "worst!"

In spite of this warning, I continued my investigations, arriving at no concrete conclusions. These theories I evolved seemed too fantastic for reality, so I delved into other mysteries, including Spiritualism. As I read books on this subject, I wondered. Was there any connection between the dead and the UFO mystery? The idea seemed stupid -- but was it? Hadn't I been a regular attendant at my Church of England before leaving home to follow life's rough path? There was this character, the "Devil." Was it too fantastic to believe that Satan was behind the discs? That they were a sign of his own activity? No, that was too damndably fantastic! And this was getting a little close to Black Magic.

I abandoned the idea. If it were fantastic, then what were these discs? There seemed to be something supernatural about them. Or did they really travel over the vast distances, through the void of space to observe the earth? And if so, why? Was it because of the Atom Bombs the United States used to blast Nagasaki and Hiroshima into near oblivion? If so, still WHY? Why didn't discs come while the ruins were still smoking? Why wait until the dead were cold and the smoke gone? I told myself it could be because of the vast distances they would have to travel through space. It couldn't be that, for if these beings had sufficient knowledge to build a craft to travel through space, wasn't it possible they could skip down here in a hurry? How? The fourth dimension? I gasped and decided this was a new possibility. It was crazy!

Satan. Black Magic. Two Japanese cities blasted to end in a cruel war. The fourth dimension. These things raced through my mind. I read all the books I could locate on Black Magic, and decided it was too evil. Evil? There had to be some connection with Satan! But what? And why? This troubled me. There had to be an answer! But what was the answer? I didn't know.

Alright, I remarked mentally, say these discs do come from another planet. Which planet was the most suspect? I began to feel like a detective.

One of a detective's jobs is to first determine and examine suspects. And my strongest feeling as to suspects involved the closest planet -- MARS. Allowing that the discs did come from Mars, the old question again arose: WHY???? Was it really because of the atom blasts? Surely the flash wasn't bright enough to be seen across all those miles. It would seem illogical that the blast or radiation effect could be detected that far away. If the closest planet might be ruled out, then what?

A good detective's job is made somewhat easier if he can be cognizant of an "inside job." Although I didn't consider myself a good detective, this thought did come to mind.

What if the discs came from somewhere CLOSER? The moon? Still unlikely. But wait, what might be closer than that? The Earth? I laughed aloud at my thoughts.

This was, indeed, impossible. Before long, I told myself, I would be seeing little green men, and then the health authorities would come and toss me into a padded cell!

Again I looked at Mars and wondered. WHAT THE BLAZES WERE THESE THINGS. I figuratively lived with the discs, and even slept with them on my mind, and constantly watched the sky. I saw them, alright, and for my efforts heard the infantile laughing of the childish scoffers.

CHAPTER FOUR
THE THING IN THE DESERT

But there was one sighting I had forgotten about. What was the thing I had seen in the Western Desert? It was November, 1941. My battalion lay in the dark, waiting for the signal which would send us forward to see and face death. A place called Sidi Rezegh. In front of us was the dark outline of the escarpment, and on top was the block-house. Nerves tensed. Safety catches were released. On our rifles, the bayonets, 17 inches of the best British steel, gave confidence. I wiped the dust from my eyes, turning my head away from the wireless at my side. I STARED BLANKLY. WHAT.......?

Behind us, and about five or six feet above the sand was an orange ball. It made no movement. I wiped the sweat from my brow, and decided it was a secret weapon of the enemy. I had no time to think any more of it. The signal came, and what remained of my battered unit went into that cruel and shocking carnage. I forgot the strange ball when I saw men fall in death, when I heard the cries of the wounded and the terrible sounds of the battle around me.

What had the orange ball been? Where had it come from? What had it been doing there. Why had it apparently been interested in we Earthmen, waiting to fight in that game of death? The Allies wouldn't claim it, and the Germans were indignant when asked if they owned it.

"Strewth, no!" declared the Kiwis.

"Nein!" cried the Germans.

So nobody owned this thing. And who would own a huge ball-like object which hung in mid-air, its glow like that of a

huge furnace. And how did it suddenly extinguish its glow and race away to the south? Where did it go? I had no ideas to put forward.

The entire mystery was frightening in its immensity, so I returned to a study of space travel, deciding this might be the best vantage point from which to attack the Enigma. I was to spend many long hours with such questions as "Why?" "Where?" and "Which?" It was most discouraging, but I gained heart and pressed on ------ a fatal mistake in view of what occurred later.

In 1952 I read a report about one Herr Linke who saw a disc in a small clearing near his home in Germany. I decided this proved that the UFOs were real, solid affairs, and not just myths. I wrote to Herr Linke, seeking further details on his close sighting, but his failure to reply caused me to wonder if he were afraid to speak about the matter, or, alternately, if he ever received my letter. I filed the report away for further reference, turning my attention to fresh reports from Australia, America, England, my own New Zealand, and other countries. It seemed there were saucers everywhere. Again the question: "What are these things?" They had been recorded in the earliest historical writings, and while there was the possibility that some of the ancient reports could have referred to heavenly bodies, some of them, quite obviously, described the very same type of UFOs we were seeing in the Twentieth Century:

The earliest report of UFOs over New Zealand was made in 1910, when a cigar-shaped object was sighted. The scoffers, no doubt, insisted it was the planet Venus, a weather balloon (if they had them at that time), or other natural objects or phenomena. But the fact remains that at 11:00 on that evening in January, 1910, a number of people in the town of Invercargill (situated at the southern end of the South Island of New Zealand) did see a cigar-shaped object at a (approximate) height of 100 feet. They also observed a door in the side of the huge object open, and a figure appear, which called out in a foreign tongue. The figure then moved back inside, the door closed, and the object sped away.

Now it is necessary to explain to the doubtful that those who saw the craft had just emerged from a local pub (the public bar where, in those old days, beer was served only until 11:00 P.M.) after a few pots of brew. The scoffer will now nod wisely, thinking he has the perfect answer: they were "shicker"! Ah, but we must spoil this theory! It is recorded that the Vicar, the Policeman, the town's Mayor, and other people of good character and importance, also saw the object, and it is unlikely that all of these particular people would have been having "a spot." So what was it? I don't know. But I am certain of two things it was not: It certainly was not Venus, nor was it a weather balloon!

CHAPTER FIVE
MAPPING THE SAUCERS

I have gone into the matter of my short tenure as an officer in the Hamilton Flying Saucer Investigation Society. When I was expelled from that organization I asked Barbara Turner to assist me in forming what was to be known as Flying Saucer Investigators. She agreed to help me. Knowing the problems of a group of individuals, with many conflicting ideas, we decided to limit the organization to only two people, Barbara and myself.

Flying Saucer Investigators vowed to tell the truth, to make known to others our views and findings, and to assist in bringing about the final solution to the Enigma. We didn't bargain for the fiendish humans about us who found a reprehensible delight in blackening our association. Soon we met frigid and frosty looks. We were shunned. And these malicious humans (?) delved into their stygian minds to find the vicious venum to throw at us. But we laughed at their pitiful efforts, often quoting an old Chinese proverb, "He who paddles in a stagnant pool will find only mud." Maybe these evil ones found that in their own minds. And in spite of this insidious talk, Barbara and I were able to effectively pursue our research.

We made contact with a U. S. researcher, Gray Barker, who became a firm friend, and assisted us in many ways, keeping us informed about the American scene as it was affected by the UFOs. He was, and still is, a dinkum cobber. Later, he showed his friendship by selecting us as two of the very few to whom a copy of a startling report was sent. We were grateful for this, and guarded the report to keep it secret as we had been requested to do. I refer here to the report on (using the name later coined by Gray in his book) Gordon Smallwood. This is not the real name of this researcher, but it will hide the real identity.

With the formation of FSI, Barbara and I would meet each evening to discuss the latest reports, and to talk at length on some new idea we had thought of during the day. Quite often our meetings lasted until 3:00 A.M., and this gave fresh fuel to the evil minded who slandered us. But these meetings were filled with great interest, and the time soon passed, leaving us with so little said and so much to say. During those early days of FSI I related to Barbara the sightings I had made, the strange experiences, and the views I had taken on UFOs. I made these reports to her as detailed as possible, so that she might have a clearer picture of the case, and as the evenings passed she became a very good pupil, and began to advance her own ideas. They were worth listening to. She made many sound suggestions, among which was a plan to draw a huge map of the world on which would be placed all the sightings we had in our possession.

"After we have all the sightings in place, Johnnie," she explained, "we hook them all up with lines to show the direction of travel. You know, the direction these things came from, and the direction in which they returned. To and from, Johnnie, is the idea."

"Whaffor?" I asked.

"By doing this," she told me, "we will have some indication as to where these things come from."

I looked at her in startled amazement. "I once thought it was possible that these things came from the Earth, but dropped it as fantastic. Now you have suggested it too! Why?" I asked her.

She lit a cigarette rather thoughtfully, looking at my collection of books. "It's obvious, isn't it?" she murmured, looking up at me.

"Obvious? What is?" I inquired, puzzled.

She sat down, and then said, "I'll explain when I draw our map. Now, do you have a huge sheet of paper?"

I located what she required and sat watching as her slim fingers guided a pencil to form the shapes of contries of the earth. It was a long job, and it was not until the following evening that we were able to look upon it as completed. As Barbara lightly tapped her teeth with her pencil, I asked, "Now, what's the next move? To mark in all the sightings?"

"Yes, Johnnie." She soon completed this section and there were the lines between each sighting. "Now, let's look at it from this angle. These saucers have to have a base, don't they? And what would be better than some vast, uninhabited part of the earth?"

"Agreed. But where?"

She returned to the map and lightly traced along the lines with her finger, a puzzled frown on her brow. "I'm not certain yet, Johnnie." Again she marked in some lines, and her hand stopped, her pencil poised like some slim pointer. "It.....it can't be!" she whispered loudly.

"What can't be, Barbara?"

"How about an area of ice, John?" she asked in a quiet voice.

I stepped to her side, close to the map, and stared at it, my eyes following the maze of lines. It was a little confusing, or I was tired, for the lines merely showed a tangle. Barbara slipped her hands into the pocket of her slacks, as a slight paleness showed beneath her make-up. "That's it, John," she said soberly.

Again I stared at the map, and with a gasp, saw what she meant. The lines had converged on Antarctica! I saw immediately the enormity of our discovery, and was all for contacting other researchers immediately.

"Wouldn't it be better to wait, Johnnie, until we have something concrete to tell them?" Barbara asked. "I know we could write to Gray and tell him, for instance, that we have a six foot long map of the world on which we've drawn a maze of lines. We could say these lines converge on Antarctica. But what would that mean? Just that we have a lot of lines on a map which converge on the south pole region." She shook her head. "No, I'm all for waiting until we really have something dinkum to offer. Think so, boy?"

Reluctantly I agreed. And this information was destined to be hidden for a long time. But that evening I agreed to wait, and we set about examing the possibility that the UFOs were based on Antarctica, asking Barbara just where she found this idea, for I had the impression she had thought in that direction before she made the map, and that it had been the final thing which had convinced her.

"From a number of things, John. One from you when you told me of the Shaver business. Another when it was quite obvious that the saucers seemed to come from and travel to the south. It added up. Like adding one and one making two." She accepted the cigarette I offered her, and then said, "Shall we study it further

"Too right, Barbs. I'm all for it," I replied eagerly. "And the first question to answer once we decide the saucers come from the pole is this: WHY?"

Barbara nodded. "Yes, John. Why? Why are they using the earth as a base? Why don't they land where they can be studied? What are they scared of? What sort of people, if they are people like us, control them? Are the saucers we see manned? Are they robots? What are they made of? What makes 'em go?" She grinned. "There sure is a lot to learn."

"That, my dear, is the understatement of the century!"

She laughed softly. "Alright, mate, where does one start? Say something silly and trust it turns out right?"

I grinned at her, and said, "Something silly, is it? Lemme see, Barbs." I thought. "Got it' One day, a long time ago, a lot of people lived at the pole, and there came upon them a terrible catastrophe in which they were frozen stiff. They were in a state of suspended animation. Thousands of years later, in a terrible war, an equally terrible bomb was exploded and the heat from it melted the ice to thaw the lost race. And along came the day when these people tried out the ships which were locked in the ice from the day when the big freeze came." I grinned. "And they live happily ever after," I laughed.

"You silly idiot, Johnnie!" giggled Barbara. "Of all the silly ideas! Deep frozen people," she grinned. "And deep frozen flying saucers!"

"Well," I remarked in mock dismay, "you did ask me to say something silly. And I did just that."

"I know. Now let's be serious. Shall we?" Her eyes twinkled. "About saucers, I mean too, you idiot."

"Alright. I'll be serious," I chuckled. "It's almost 1954, and as soon as the New Year comes, I'll be serious for a whole year. Howzat?"

"Bet you can't."

"On. It's a bet, Barbs!" I grinned at her. Had we known what the year of 1954 had in store for us, I venture to suggest that we would have forgotten not only our bet, but everything to do with UFOs! It was to be a year of terror. Of horror and fear.

CHAPTER SIX
ANCIENT PEOPLES AND THE UFO

New Year's day, 1954, was behind us, and we commenced a serious study of the Antarctica theory. As we did so we began to see the terrible possibilities of this idea. Could it be that the saucers were literally on New Zealand's own doorstep? And if so, what was their purpose in being there? How did they manage to survive the intense cold?

I mentioned to Barbara the possibility that Admiral Byrd had seen something of the UFOs when he had been on his polar expeditions.

"Yes, he must have seen something strange down there, John. It has been rumored, hasn't it, that he was officially silenced before he could tell WHAT, though? Pity, really."

I formed new ideas as we talked of Antarctica. "I believe the polar region to be mountainous, and it is quite likely that there are plenty of places where a UFO, or a number of them, could hide away from the eyes of even the most careful expeditions. It's a big thing to study, isn't it?"

Barbara settled back in her chair, frowning a little as she toyed with her cigarette. "But why do the UFOs want to hang around at the pole, Johnnie?"

"Wish I knew. If I could answer that, Barbs, I could answer the entire case. Couldn't I?" I paused and lit up a fresh cigarette. "Of course it could have something to do with the ice cap. It's diminishing in size, isn't it?"

"Yes," nodded Barbara. "And that could be part of the answer, couldn't it? These saucer people, if we can call them that, know the manner in which the pole is melting and have come here to study the effects. A cold idea, but possible. Anyway, if our ice cap was to melt that much, then heaven help us! It would cause our planet to topple, wouldn't it? It wouldn't take much to make it topple either, flinging us into oblivion." Then she added quietly, "Not a pleasant thought, is it?"

"No," I replied, "it's a nasty thought. Anyway, keep talking, you might come up with something really startling."

(Editor's note: We believe John and Barbara were in error about the melting. To our knowledge, there is some indication that the North Pole is melting slightly, and that ice is building up at the South Pole. The latter condition, so states engineer Hugh A. Brown, could lead to a toppling and change of axis of the earth -- G.B.)

She nodded and then grinned happily. "Keep talking, the boy says! See, just think what our nasty minded friends are now saying about our being here together. And we are just talking as we should be. What a let-down for them, eh? Where was I? Oh, yes. This idea of the earth toppling might not be so silly, you know, after reading Velikovsky's book. He related there how some cosmic upheaval affected the earth all those thousands of years ago, and how that mammoth was found in Siberia with grass still in its mouth."

She paused for a moment, and then continued, "Of course this may not have anything to to do with the Antarctica idea, but it's in the same category, isn't it? Anyway, whatever happened to that mammoth was so sudden that it was deep frozen in a split second of time."

She snapped her fingers expressively. "Bang! Just like that! Quick. Fast. Too fast to understand what had turned you into an iceberg." She was now smiling eagerly as she snapped her lighter, drawing smoke into her lungs.

"Now, allowing that the earth is in a similar danger, is it so silly to believe the saucer people are coming here to see just what is happening to us? That the UFOs are really space vehicles used by Martian scientists?" she asked seriously.

"Yes, it's possible," I agreed. "But why whould they come all that way just to see us meet our doom?

"Because, maybe, they were once earth dwellers," Barbara answered calmly.

Barbara said this so seriously and so knowingly that

I started. Not that the idea was so blasted startling, but it must have been the way she said it. It was almost as if someone other than Barbara were talking. I believe that was the moment that I, in looking back, first noticed some change taking place in Barbara, a change that was indicative of untold suffering she, directly, and I, indirectly, would undergo. I wish our association had been cut off at that time, but what is done cannot be undone.

I remember that I commented enthusiastically:

"They....hey, dicken! That's too flaming fantastic, Barbs!"

"It is?" she inquired, a trifle archly.

"Fair dinkum, kid, you're just being funny," I told her with a grin.

Barbara raised her eyebrows, and asked me with mock aloofness, "Am I? Well, you like to study old ruins, don't you?"

"Old buildings? Yes, I like to study them. Why?"

"Well, do you know where the Aztecs went?"

"The Aztecs? Why they just up and......" I stopped. Where the devil DID they go? I poured a glass of beer, chuckled and said, "To be honest, Barbara, I forgot to ask the last one I saw."

Barbara frowned at me. "Oh! Do be a little serious."

"You're right, Barb. Alright, I just dunno what happened to them."

"You see? Now listen to me, Johnnie. The Aztecs were a race of very clever people, and erected fine temples which the modern builder would have quite a time with. They made a deep study of science, and the scientific side of life, seeing that the earth was doomed to destruction, or at the least, its living beings were in danger of destruction. They could forsee this terrible catastrophe, and immediately went about leaving the earth to escape death; and after they departed, this deathly cold struck, deep-freezing any living creatures remaining. And it was swift, too."

"Then you believe the Aztecs lived here on earth as a civilized race when the mighy mammoth roamed the earth?

"Exactly."

"And providing this theory of your's is correct, what happened to those who couldn't escape?"

She shrugged her shoulders. "I have no idea, really. Bit by bit we can look into that."

"Where's the proof that all this happened?"

"None, old thing. But there are those temples in a verdant jungle. So where did the blokes and their sheilas go? They just couldn't say, 'Oh, blow this, mate! Let's go look for another world!'" She chuckled.

"You silly idiot," I laughed.

She grinned, and then said, "Let's be serious, eh? They must have gone somewhere. And there's the statues on Easter Island. What happened to those who quarried the stone and cut the blocks to shape? Something caused them to down tools in a flaming hurry and bolt like blue blazes. Where to? Why? What caused them to leave? Was there something to fear here on this planet?"

"Granting they left as you say, why should their descendants want to return to study our mode of living?"

"As I said before, Johnnie, the earth may be approaching some sort of catastrophe, and they are clinically interested in the means of our escape. To them, we earth people are just guinea pigs in a matter of life and death."

"A very cold thought," I remarked grimly.

"We have to be coldly analytical in such investigations, and all our research, John."

"I grant that, Barbara. But all this must have happened countless thousands of years ago! And that being so, where did you, me, the other people of this earth come from? I mean the inhabitants who escaped were alright, but what of those who didn't escape? Naturally, they died in the catastrophe, and so there was no life left. There were no white men, no Indians, no Chinese, or anyone else. Where did we all come from if there was no life remaining to reproduce?"

"To answer that, Johnnie, we must go back to the Bible, to the time of Adam and Eve."

"Why them, Barbara?"

"Because, Johnnie, they were the first to arrive after

the terror. I believe that Adam and Eve were two people who lived on another planet. Their home was a place where there was no sin, no crime, and where everyone lived a perfect existence. The Bible tells us that Eve picked a forbidden apple, and to bring that crime up to date, let us say she committed some crime against the society in which she lived. They were punished, and to be sure they didn't commit any further crimes on their own planet, they were exiled to earth, naked and alone. They were the first to return after the catastrophe, and soon set about making a home on a strange planet. Of course, I refuse to believe they were the mother and father of the earth people who today inhabit this planet, but they did have children, and one of them returned to the other planet to find himself a mate. It's obvious that all these stories have some basis in fact, and regardless of whether the is Biblical or not, one must look closer to find what might really have happened. To find the truth is rather simple, or at least I should say, I think it is simple. All you have to do is study the old story and bring it up to date.

"Go on," I urged, fascinated not only by her remarks, but rather puzzled by her erudition. These long discourses were unlike my friend. It seemed as though "something had come over her," so to speak.

"It could have happened just as I say. And the different races? The white. Black. Red. Yellow. Each is quite different in color and outlook, and therefore could have come from different planets. Maybe they came from planets at little and grea distances from the sun, which might account for the skin colors."

"But are you inferring that these different races, and of course, Adam and Eve, came from our own Universe?"

"Perhaps. But what was to stop their coming from another universe?"

"Nothing at all," I replied. "But what have the UFOs to do with Adam and Eve?"

"How do you think our naked couple got here? They could hardly have walked, could they?" she grinned.

"Hardly! So you believe they came by disc?"

"Yes, and to get here, maybe they used the moon as a sort of stepping stone."

"And what do you think about the races who use the UFOs now?" I asked her.

Barbara looked thoughtful, and admitted, "I don't know." "Of course," she then added, "there may be two groups of them at work. One bunch the goody-goods, and B the baddies. The good space people wants us to live a decent life in spite of their clinical interest in us, while the bad ones are out to make us live a lecherous life."

"That's something of what Shaver said," I advised her.

"And so I have said it."

"But what has all this to do with the ice cap down below on our back doorstep?" I inquired.

"Nothing. I just think up these ideas on the hope it will give us a new lead, that's all," she murmured.

"Well, forget your 'goodie' and 'baddie' space people idea. Your first thought was more interesting."

Barbara smiled. "Yes, I like it too. At the same time, Johnnie, we should look at this idea of bad and good, or good and evil, whichever sounds right."

"I've tried that one."

"What, Johnnie?"

"Good and evil, of course," I explained.

She grinned at me. "I know. You said you'd had a pretty wild time at the war."

I laughed at her audacious grin. "I was talking about UFO research! Not that kind of evil, you idiot!"

"Right-o, mate. But I still think it's worth thinking about." She looked at her watch. "Strewth! It's almost half past one! I'm away on a fast camel! More talk tomorrow night, Johnnie. Goodnight, mate," she smiled.

CHAPTER SEVEN
R.A.F. REPORTS OBJECT

When we met the next evening, Barbara seemed to be more of her "old self" again. I mention this partly in light of what you will read later, and partly in defense of Barbara. Barbara had impressed me as a sweet, kind, innocent girl -- that was the reason I could work with her, even late of nights, without feeling guilty of anything that the rumor-mongers no doubt spread. There are, indeed, such things as love, and physical desire. But transcending the latter, and maybe even love, is another feeling, that of deep friendship of pure nature. That is how I felt about her.

We studied reports of "little green men" allegedly seen in remote parts of the United States. Barbara asked me what I thought about them.

"Just a lot of rot," I growled.

"Oh, I don't know, Johnnie," she remonstrated; "There may be some truth in the reports!"

"Why," I frowned.

"Well, look at this one," and she held out a clipping. "It says here that a chap saw one of the little men near his mine. The small bloke wanted some water, it seems."

I lit a cigarette and said, grumpily, "So did the bloke who claimed he saw the little character! Only he wanted some water for his flaming whisky!"

"Don't be so nasty, Johnnie!" admonished Barbara. "Lots of people see things which are never explained! And never believed either!"

"I know that, my dear," I replied, and then told her again

of the strange thing I saw at Sidi Rezegh in 1941.

"And did the other soldiers see it too?"

"Never heard if they did," I answered. "After the stoush was over, we who were left talked about the fighting, and of those who hadn't made it. At that time the silly thing in the sky just didn't seem to be important. Certainly someone else must have seen it. But out of my battalion more than a third were killed or wounded. If others did see it, my guess is that they, like I, just didn't think it was important enough to talk about at that time."

"Strange, alright," remarked Barbara. "It makes one think, doesn't it, of that report in the British newspaper of the object which the authorities said was a weather balloon."

The report had been published in THE DAILY MIRROR, dated November 19, 1953. Banner headlines shouted:

MYSTERY "SPOT" SEEN ON LONDON RADAR SCREEN
TWO R.A.F. PILOTS REPORT "OBJECT"

> Radar screens of a London Anti-aircraft unit have twice recently picked up mysterious objects in the sky. The most recent was on Tuesday, when Sergeant-Major Ernest Stead, a radar instructor, was making a routine check at the headquarters of the 265 Regiment Heavy A.F., at Lee Green, Lewisham.
>
> With four civilian helpers, he got on the screen "a very strong target" at a height of about 60,000 feet. The object was moving slowly, and it gradually went out of range.
>
> Sergeant-Major Stead reported the incident to his adjutant, Captain Fowler, who told Brigade headquarters. Captain Fowler said last night, "It is impossible to say what the object was. Because of the fog, it could not be seen through the sighting telescope, but the strength of the signal seemed to indicate that the object was of colossal size."

The report continued with details of a sighting made by Sergeant Waller, on November 3, 1953, about the same time of the day. In his report to Captain Fowler, Sergeant Waller said,

> "We got a very strong target between 2:30 and 3:15 P.M. The signal was extremely strong. I estimated the object's height at 61,000 feet. It was stationary for

some time, then moved slowly away and gradually went out of range. It disappeared at about 43,000 feet. As soon as I lost it from the screen I went out to see if I could see it. Through the sighting telescope I saw a round or spherical object, a brilliant white in color, still stationary. Although it looked small through the telescope, it must have been of great size to be visible at that height."

Two R.A.F. pilots stationed at West Malling, Kent, saw an object that they could not identify on the same day as Sergeant Waller, but about four hours earlier.

The following day it seemed the authorities were making an all-out effort to ridicule this latest sighting. One headline read, "IT MIGHT HAVE BEEN A BALLOON," and on Page 2 there appeared a large headline:

FLYING SAUCER WAS A BIG BALLOON

The "flying saucer" reported by army radar men on November 3 was a balloon, the Air Ministry said last night.

It was said to have been sent up by meterological men from an Air Ministry weather station at Crawley, Sussex. Said an Air Ministry spokesman: "It has been established that there was a balloon up at that time and in that area, and there can be little doubt that this was the object sighted."

The object reported and tracked by the radar men was also reported by the crew of a Vampire jet fighter. But the man who tracked the "saucer"....was unconvinced:

"I would never have been able to see a balloon 12 miles away if it had been only 12 feet across, as the Ministry says it was. Suppose it was a balloon we saw, what was it the R.A.F. saw? They reported it at 10:20 A.M., but according to the Ministry that balloon did not go up until 2:00 P.M."

After we had read this report, Barbara remarked that it was strange how the Air Ministry had avoided any mention of the object reported on November 19. I pointed out that they had made some half-hearted attempt to ridicule this too, and read her a small item: "IT MIGHT HAVE BEEN A BALLOON. A possible explanation for the 'mystery spot' on the radar screen....was given by the Air

Ministry last night. A spokesman said it could have been a weather balloon."

There were a couple of other lines saying that balloons carry a metal tail which is designed to give a strong "echo."

It was interesting to note that in this case, as in contrast to the previous one, the Ministry said it was a "possible explanation." Nothing definite about it. Just "possible."

"The authorities have spoken!" mocked Barbara. "There we have the solution to the UFOs! You and I, Johnnie, are just wasting our time, as are so many other researchers throughout the world. We should have more common sense than to mistake the UFO for a common weather balloon! And to think that over the last couple of hundred years there have been weather balloons drifting about the sky! And in a lot of cases the said balloons even had the audacity to go against the wind! Anyway, I always understood weather balloons were something new. Something that our ancient forefathers didn't know anything about! But, there you are, Johnnie, the UFOs are just weather balloons, and not even the pilots of the fighter planes know any better!" she added in deep scorn.

"Those pilots who see these so-called balloons will have to be better trained," I said. "To think that it's youngsters like them who will defend the Commonwealth in the event of another war! Maybe we should let the authorities pilot the planes? They know what's a weather balloon and what's something else!"

"Yes," nodded Barbara. "And just how long will these jack-booted officials go on with their stupidity? Why won't they admit the truth?"

"Maybe they don't know any better, Barbara."

"And they are allowed to make such childish statements?"

"But they have no real answer to the mystery. And to hide their ignorance, these so-called learned men jump to their feet and wave their arms in the air as they make their idiotic press releases! They're too afraid to admit they have no idea of what the UFOs are!"

Barbara smiled at my harsh tone, and said, "But when that object was sighted from the Dak, the local authorities must have decided to ignore it, eh? There was one which no one has explained. Of course," she said, with a taunting smile, "it was just a weather balloon, wasn't it, Johnnie?"

The report appeared in the EVENING POST of January 11, 1952, and read:

AIR-TO-AIR SIGHTING OF UNKNOWN OBJECT NEAR KUITI

The first recorded air-to-air sighting of an unknown object in New Zealand occurred at 9:27 last night. The co-pilot of a National Airways Corporation DC-3, First Officer K. G. Bond, watched a brilliant reddish-orange light move steadily across the path of the liner. He thinks it was too low and travelling too slowly to have been a meteor.

The Dakota at the time was on its way from Wellington to Auckland, and 15 miles west of Kuiti.

First Officer Bond at once checked by radio with Air Traffic Control in Wellington and was told that no aircraft were flying in the Wellington or Auckland control areas.

When he was startled by the light dead ahead, First Officer Bond had just looked up from checking his instruments in the cockpit.

"It was brighter than any meteor and was moving from west to east in a straight line," he said today. "It was about the size of Venus in the sky and had a definite tail of color. Meteors usually travel in a curved path and speed up. They go much faster than this light travelled. It seemed to be about one and a half miles in front and at 8,000 feet -- 1,000 feet higher than the aircraft. But it must have been farther away as the light would have moved towards the starboard wingtip in the 45 seconds I watched it."

The Captain was called to the cockpit, but the light had then disappeared.

"It was fairly cloudy below, but was clearer towards Tauranga and Rotorua," added First Officer Bond. "I hope somebody over there saw it. I always regarded reports of 'flying saucers' with skepticism. I am not prepared to say this was a 'flying saucer,' but I am convinced now there is something in the reports."

I remarked to Barbara, "And there is another case where a reliable pilot has seen one of these things while in flight. I suppose one could safely say that it was not a balloon? That the stock reply is a little out of the line of sanity in this report?"

"Maybe K. G. wasn't feeling well, and was just seeing things, Johnnie," she grinned. "Isn't that another stock answer? That we who do see these UFOs are just seeing things?"

"There are lots of excuses and explanations," I answered.

"Maybe, of course, he saw a weather balloon? Or was it the planet Venus? Amazing, y'know, the antics that these weather balloons and poor old Venus get up to! Of course, Johnnie, like our cobber, K. G. Bond, we're just plain silly! The very idea of you and I actually believing in flying saucers!" she said in a mocking tone. She stared at her cigarette for a moment, and then went on, still derisively: "We must be silly, y'know, to mistake a UFO for a common weather balloon. Can't understand how we could be so flaming stupid, can you? Why even that cigar thing we saw last week was only the planet Venus in disguise!"

"If the pilot was tired and seeing things, why wasn't he grounded? Why allow him to fly a liner and risk his passengers' lives?"

"For the very same reason as were other pilots left to fly after sighting a UFO," Barbara told me aggressively. "The authorities wouldn't be game to ground these men' So they allow them to fly, knowing full well there is something more there than they care to admit. If, and I say if, these things are just weather balloons, how is it that the said thing can travel against the wind? How is it that a balloon can travel at great speeds? Stop and start? Reverse its direction of flight? Of course," she cried in a contemptous tone, "there might be one of those official types inside it, eh?" She laughed. "And in both cases, there would be a lot of hot air!"

"You're becoming a fair dinkum researcher, aren't you," I chuckled.

CHAPTER EIGHT
BARBARA'S STRANGE ACTIONS

"Well," replied Barbara, warmly," I do have some brains, Johnnie! Anyway, let's forget these idiots." She was silent for a moment, and then asked, "Johnnie, what is down at Antarctica? Ice, I realize. But what I mean is this: What did Admiral Byrd see? Was it the UFOs in their true plane?"

"Yes," I murmured, What did he see?" It was a most interesting question, I realized, as I looked toward my companion.

She sat in her chair, relaxed, with a deep, thoughtful expression in her eyes. I momentarily forgot the UFOs, and allowed my thoughts to dwell on this attractive young woman. Young, attractive looks, a slim figure, a deep sense of humor, and rather clownish when she was happy, and that was most of the time. She was lost in thought as I stared at her. Her lips were slightly parted in a sort of eagerness, and I wondered just what was going on in her mind. Was she thinking of some new idea that affected the research we were doing? Or was she thinking of other things?

As far as I knew, she had no boy friends, and since she had been spending almost every evening at my home, discussing the saucers, I figured she had no interest in any boy, at least for the present.

It did seem wrong to me that she should be wasting her hours talking with someone much older than herself; she should be out with a boy, talking of her future, of love, marriage and children. I smiled inwardly. She would make someone happy eventually, and later be a young New Zealand mother.

I reflected on myself, when I had been her age. I had spent those similar years with a deadly rifle in my hands, fighting a war that was to bring peace and freedom to mankind, whatever

G. DUPLANTIER

his race or creed. I felt bitter for a moment. Where was the peace? Where was the happiness of living? Again I saw the erupting countryside, the sand of the desert stretching far into the distance, the snarling stutter of machine guns, the sharp crack of a rifle. Youth. It had gone in that hell! We went away as mere boys, and those of us who were lucky came back as old men of twenty-four and twenty-five. Youth was lost. And in its loss we had known only hell!

I looked again at Barbara. She and the boys her age were being spared all that. Despite my bitter feelings of a few moments past, I could feel glad for Barbara and them.

She looked up at me, the smile fading from her lips. "What...what's wrong, Johnnie?" she whispered, leaning forward.

"Just thinking," I replied. "Anyway, we were talking about UFOs."

She ignored my mention of the saucers, and asked, "But you said you were thinking. Of what?" she insisted.

I didn't want to talk about it, but to satisfy her, I said, "Of life. The years we lost at the war, and all that."

"But wasn't it an education...in some ways?"

"Yes, I agree. But it doesn't bring back the lost years, does it? There's thousands of us, Kiwis, Americans, Australians, English and so on. So many who wonder what it was all about." I lit a cigarette. "However, that's a man's job, and now it's over, little one."

A very strange look came over Barbara's face, one I had never noticed before. It was almost as if her features had hardened. Maybe it was the way the light caught her face as she turned slightly, but I imagined she suddenly looked much older.

"Yes, a man's job," she nodded. "Gee, I'm glad I'm a girl. We have more fun. We can make any boy we like go half silly. I like to be kissed. And I like to tease boys." She grinned.

I was taken aback by suddenly facing an entirely new facet of her personality. I could only mumble, "What do you mean?"

"Lots of ways," she grinned again. "With a partly open shirt. Brief shorts. All that." Her smile turned more sensual.

I laughed nervously. "You're a scamp," I chided, "Even

dressed as you are." A fear played on my mind, as I thought of something more to say, something that would get the subject back on our research.

Then she said something that for the first time made me fully realize that something had somehow "taken over" Barbara, that a new type of personality was somehow coming through.

"Why? Frightened of me?" she mocked.

I said nothing.

"I'd like to sit here naked. Like me to?" She whispered the latter in a very suggestive manner.

"Please, Barbara," I pleaded, trying to find some way out of the embarrassing situation. Suddenly she herself switched the subject, but I could detect the same strange look on her face.

"Ice," she remarked. "Ice reflects light, doesn't it, Johnnie?"

It was as though her outrageous idea of undressing was suddenly gone, and had never been thought of.

"Yes, and in a mass like the southern polar cap it would act like a huge mirror."

She was silent for a moment, and then said, "I'm going to let my thoughts run wild and see what I come up with."

"Alright," I said guardedly.

"The ice reflects light just like a huge mirror, throwing light into the sky. Light, in turn, plays some funny tricks on the human eye. And it could be possible that the ice causes us to see funny things, too." She lit a cigarette and looked at me. "The UFOs are above the earth observing. Crossing their own flight paths. Minding their own business. And the ice at the south pole is reflecting an image like a mirror. I don't know sufficient about light to make this any clearer, nor to explain in technical terms what I have in mind, but I think you will see what I'm getting at. The UFOs might be anywhere above the pole and the ice captures the image, reflecting it so we can see it all."

I took up the idea. "Yes, and the fact that the UFOs are on the ice would cause your idea to work just the same. Man can bend light, and so can nature. What you are suggesting is that the UFOs are caused by a mirage. Possible, I agree."

"I think it is feasible, too, Johnnie. But first we must believe that the UFOs are either on the ice or somewhere above it. But I like to believe they are using the pole as a sort of base."

A new theory was forming in my mind, but for the moment I returned to Barbara's theory. "But, why do they insist on congregating at the pole? Why not, say, the Sahara? Or, again, the upper reachers of the Amazon?"

"The Sahara is too open," Johnnie," Barbara said. "No, I think the ice cap is the better place. You see, there may be some mineral down there that they are interested in. How do you like that?"

"Again, quite feasible. But there's a hell of a lot more to it all than that."

"H'm," nodded Barbara. "I see that," she agreed, slowly pressing the cigarette in the ash tray. "I'll think about it in bed. Now I must go, Johnnie."

I walked to the gate with her, and it seemed that once again Barbara was the same innocent young person she had been before her strange conversation of that evening.

I opened the gate told her to sleep well. She paused, momentarily, and I stood there, just a bit embarrassed by the silence.

Suddenly she threw her arms around my waist, pressed her head to my shoulder, and whispered, "Help me, Johnnie, help me!"

Before I could ask her what was wrong she had released me and was running down the walkway.

CHAPTER NINE
THE PEOPLE OF THE POLES

As I lay in bed, I thought more about Barbara's strange attitude. Had her delving into the UFO secret affected her in some odd way? My first thoughts were to end the association immediately, and to do my research alone.

Then I thought of her parting remark, "Help me!" and my decision changed. Barbara was a dear friend. None but the purest thoughts had passed my mind as we had worked the evenings together. Throughout our association a genuine affection had developed in my heart for her. If she were in the need of help, maybe it was because I had introduced her to this weird subject of saucers.

I knew Barbara could come to no harm, physically, from me. If something else were harming her, maybe I should try and do something about it. So I decided to continue the association, at least until I knew just what was wrong.

The next morning a rather strange new theory started running through my mind -- a theory which to some degree repelled me. I tried putting it from my mind, but it continued to annoy me all day. I decided not to mention this theory to Barbara, particularly because of what had passed the night before.

When we met that evening Barbara appeared quite her old self, and she began our work by again getting out the world map and going over it.

"I'm more convinced than ever that the saucers are based at the South Pole," she began, then noticing what she later described as a "blank look" on my face, she asked, with some concern, "Why, Johnnie, what's wrong?"

I said nothing, and just sat there, staring, I remember,

at the ashtray, which had two or three cigarette remains in it. I felt remarkably light, though not dizzy. I knew I was not drunk, for I had not even had a glass of beer yet. I really cannot describe the sensation I felt, but the best way to put it is to say that it seemed that somebody or something was staring at me -- yet staring deep inside me.

"What's wrong? You're not acting right?" she continued.

I began speaking, as if I had very little control of what I was saying. I can remember what was happening very well, for I can recall what I said, almost word for word. Barbara continued to look at me in amazement as I spoke in what she later described as "more of a monotone" than my usual voice, which I certainly do not believe is usually monotonous:

"For a long time we've talked about Antarctica. We've decided it is from here that the UFOs come. I believe this to be correct, but not all come from there, of course. To explain, we must return to a time many thousands of years ago. Maybe to the time you spoke of when you mentioned the Aztecs. Possibly even before that, too. Back to an age when a very advanced race lived on Earth. To a time when there was a warning of an impending catastrophe.

"The holocaust struck quickly, and those who were left made their home at the present south pole. I would suggest that Queen Maud Land was their home. They settled down to rebuild their life as they had once known it, and as the years passed the cold began to recede, but not at the pole. There it remained frozen and desolate. It was there that this race of people began to wear clothing, and this was to keep their bodies warm, and not for the sake of modesty.

"After they had lived there for many years, and the cold had released the earth, except for the pole, another race arrived from far away, making the previous race their slaves. The newcomers were sadistic and lecherous, using the women as their toys, the men as their workers. The newcomers arrived here in the type of spacecraft we now see in our skies. For some reason they settled at the pole, shunning the outside world, maybe because of its lack of living things. An age passed by, and the children, born of the lecherous knowledge of the Earth women, became the masters. I refer to the male offspring, of course, and they continued their lustful actions upon the female offspring, producing more young. They worked and died, and the race continued. Maybe these people, if that is the correct term, are the lost race we have heard so much about.

"It is possible that they were the ones who built the

pyramids, the ones who carved the huge monoliths on Easter Island. It is possible that here we have the two races referred to by Shaver. I believe too this theory would account for the reason that UFOs have been seen over many centuries. The one part that I have no answer for is, of course, why they haven't attacked us, taking over the earth."

As I spoke, I gradually came out of the "trance" I seemed to be under. Barbara apparently forgot about my strange manner, in her fascination for what I had been saying, for she broke in with a question.

"But why should they want to take over the earth, Johnnie?" she asked, a little fearfully.

"I'm not certain, Barbara. But the answer might be hidden behind a rather cryptic question, 'What color is Saturday?' And when you answer that, well, you might well have the answer to our puzzle."

"Yes, I see that. Now you say these people of the earth wore clothing only when they went to the pole. Do you mean that in their normal life, prior to the catastrophe, they went about naked?"

"Yes. And there may be some connection there between these people and Adam and Eve. Although it could be a very remote possibility," I explained. "There is no doubt that clothes were used in those far away days as a sort of decoration, and not to hide the human body as they are today. We read of the ancient Greeks stripping to take part in their athletic games, and this seems to show, quite obviously, that clothes were only a form of decoration. This is shown in the pictures found in the tombs of Egypt. The slaves are depicted as naked, and in many cases, the daughters of the priests and other high ranking ones, the pictures show a girl in a skirt-like garment. Her breasts are always bare. But returning to our earlier talk, the race which settled at the pole had no need for clothes, it not being until they settled at the pole that the need did arise."

"What about the girls," Barbara asked with concern. "Were they safe, do you think, without clothing?"

"I believe there was a law in their community which protected the women -- either a moral code or a punitive code. To have contravened it would have been a most serious thing. I believe this has something to do with the Biblical account of Adam and Eve."

"It could," agreed Barbara. "Now, what would you say

as to how your ice people appear? What are they like in build? In general appearance?"

"The first race was like us. Just normal looking humans, but there could have been a nuclear explosion to have caused the catastrophe, and the blast could have changed their glands, and the functioning of them. Radiation could have made a lot of changes, and so could the attacking races who came later. As the women gave birth to their children, they produced something far different from themselves. The attacking race could have been something quite frightening to us of today, and definitely foreign to Earth people. I can picture something with a large head, a big body, and webbed feet."

"Why the webbed feet?"

"Because they lived, and still live, in the sea."

"Why the sea, though," Barbara asked.

"They probably lived in the sea back on their own planet before coming to Earth. They could have been half-man, if that is the word I want, and half fish-come-animal."

"Like a satyr?" shuddered Barbara.

"Yes, like a satyr," I nodded. "And there again is another fairy tale which could have a basis in fact. The story of the satyrs and the nymphs. Maybe the satyrs were the attacking races, and the nymphs were the Earth people."

"And the nymphs always lost, didn't they?"

"Yes, the satyr always caught them......"

"What a horrible thought," Barbara whispered.

"One only need look at Clodion's work of art, 'Nymph and Satyr,' to appreaciate what happened to the women when they were caught by the satyrs! They were slaves to the things; Clodion's work is unmercifully explicit, as the nymph pours wine into the open mouth of her violator."

"And now we believe these two were those who once occupied the earth?

"If you wish to let your imagination go that far, Barbs, I told her."

I remembered her asking for help the previous evening,

as she asked, with some noticeable agitation, "Then you believe that these so-called fairy tales have a basis in fact?"

"I do," I said earnestly. "And I also believe that the controllers of most of the present UFOs are the descendants of those very ones the fairy tales tell us of. I say 'fairy tales,' meaning, naturally, stories which seem to belong in the realm of fantasy."

"This is all very interesting," Johnnie, she said in in a quiet voice, "but rather frightening, just the same."

"Still want to be a UFO researcher?" I asked her lightly.

"YES!" was her emphatic reply.

Then she looked toward the floor, and said in a very low, halting, almost sobbing voice:

"Johnny, are you thinking.......are you thinking that one of those blokes might.....might rape me too!"

"Now, Barbara, that's too fantastic to entertain," I answered calmly and seriously.

She tried to smile. "I hope you're right, Johnnie."

CHAPTER TEN
THE VISITOR

I will not attempt to explain the happenings I will now relate. Perhaps one more versed than I in the fields of hidden knowledge may be able to make some pattern or sense out of it. I can only relate it the way it actually happened.

I go back to a continuation of our discussion on the same evening.

"To continue with this theory," I stated, "the UFO characters keep in touch with the outside world by mental telepathy, and by that means they know just what we do, and what is happening on any given part of the earth. And it is through that means that some researchers have met with trouble."

"Al Bender, too?"

"In a way. But I reckon his visitors were as human as you and me. Maybe he had similar thoughts as ours? Would you agree with that?"

"Yes," answered Barbara. "But where do these strange odors come into it all? The strange things we heard from America? What of them?"

(Editor's note: At the time this book was written by John Stuart, the book by Albert K. Bender had not yet been distributed -- G.B.)

"Maybe it has something to do with a possibility that they travel via the astral plane. The smells? Well, that could be their natural odor."

"But," remonstrated Barbara, "the idea that they might travel via the astral plane is getting very close to spiritualism."

"I know. But we are dealing with a race far in advance of us," I replied seriously.

"But, that means that old Satan is wrapped up in this business!" she cried out.

"Well, it is possible, too, Barbara. Anything is possible in this business."

I tensed. I saw the same hard look steal over Barbara's features which I had noticed the night before. Her innocent face steeled into a cold, sensuous thing.

"Anything is possible, eh?" she asked, teasingly; and then as a wild and tempestuous expression came in her eyes, she taunted, "Even letting me sit here unclothed?" She chuckled impishly.

I was frightened. "Later, eh?" I replied, not knowing quite what to say.

"I'll keep you to that," she murmured, almost happily.

I tried to get her mind off what certainly, I thought, must be some sort of an evil possession. I continued:

"As I was saying, anything is possible. I too believe that the UFO controllers can project their inner-selves to any point they care to. It's easy, really, because I learned the use of such a power myself."

"You can what!" gasped Barbara, staring at me.

"Project my innerself to any point I wish," I explained. "I can sit here and, say, visit you. It's my inner-self which goes out."

"And you can see just as if you were really there?"

"Yes."

"Gee," she grinned. "That'd be nice, wouldn't it?" She laughed softly as if the idea were filled with some deep secret amusement. "But coming back to Al Bender. Who were his visitors? Were they space men?"

"No," I explained, "I feel they were definitely human. They could have been from his own Government, or they might have been priests from some church or other. Either would interpret the fear he felt if his findings were against the safety of his country. And of the world, too, possibly."

"That means then that he may have had the actual solu tion to the UFOs?"

"Exactly, Barbara. If it's not the actual solution, then it must be something pretty big! But whatever he knew was sufficient to cause his silence, and sufficient to cause him to feel ill for some days after the visit."

"But," remarked Barbara, "if his theory was the correct one, why did it make him sick only after his visitors had left? Isn't it more likely that it was something he was told which made him ill? A warning of some sort? But I find it hard to interpret his sickness (The strange sensuous look had now left Barbara's face). Why should it make him ill? Did his findings mean some shocking cruelty from the UFOs? Did the fear affect the safety of his wife?"

"Al was single when he said the three men visited him."

"No," Barbara went on, "there's a point there that we haven't got on to. I seem to feel it was something Bender just couldn't say, something he might even be ashamed to say. Something along the lines we have been talking about. I am certain of one thing -- Bender is not a crook. He's telling the truth about being silenced, but he hasn't told everything and I don't think he ever will tell everything."

"Whatever it was, Barb, it was pretty grim. Something he could not fight against, and something he would have to face helplessly," I added, as I looked at her. "And you can rest in peace knowing that whatever it is we have to fear, I'll do all in my power to offer you protection, just as I would my own wife. If I can, as a man, stop your being harmed, then I'll do all possible."

Tears came to her eyes, as she said, "Thank you, Johnnie It's nice to know you have said all that. I've never had any fears since we began this research, but the time might come when I'll know fear. But the fact that you are near to help will lighten the load that may weigh in my heart and upon my mind." She wiped her eyes, and added, "I'll be all right, Johnnie. They won't try to harm me."

"They won't try to harm me." Was this a deep faith she had in me? Or was it that she really felt that there were no dangers? Whatever she felt in her heart, it was wrong, for she was in danger. A shocking danger. But one we never foresaw, and therefore had no defense against. And as we did not know what those future days and nights held for us, we calmly went ahead with our research into the UFOs, carefully analyzing each report, adding more views and thoughts to our theory.

Prior to the first serious attack upon us, an incident took place which, like, so many others, is unexplainable. Although it was a much different type of interference from that which we would experience later, it is probably linked to the other matters and must therefore be added here.

It was a warm evening, as I sat across from my companion talking of the possibility that Mars might be involved in the UFO business. When I saw Barbara suddenly stare, partly in fear, over my head, I turned and saw a stranger standing almost behind me, a soft smile on his rather effeminate face. I sprang to my feet, seeing that Barbara was sitting quite still. I asked the man who he was and how he got into my home?

A soft smile was his reply, and at last he told us he was a space man, and had called to add his words to the warning I had received some months before. I was shaken by this visit, and found myself just standing there, staring at and studying my visitor.

I put his age at about 30 years. He was tall, and slimly built. But I was not fooled with this slim appearance, realizing that there were well-developed muscles beneath the black suit he wore. His skin was such that any girl would have been envious of it. He was tanned to a deep tan color, and his hair was quite long, being very fair. His eyes were a soft blue and held a friendly expression. It seemed that there was nothing to fear from him, and it was apparent that Barbara saw nothing to disturb her, for she still sat in her chair.

The stranger again told us to leave well enough alone, and to cease our investigations. His eyes moved to Barbara, and he pointed out that she would be in danger if we persisted. With this warning still in our ears, the stranger vanished from view.

I poured two large brandies, and stared at my young companion. She was looking fixedly at the spot where the stranger had stood, her eyes filled with amazement. Then she turned to stare at me, and I saw her hand was shaking slightly. I suggested that she had better go home, and agreed to accompany her part of the way.

CHAPTER ELEVEN
THE SECRET OF THE SPHINX

The following evening we discussed the strange affair, and tried to explain it away to ourselves as a hoax or prank of some sort, but I'm afraid we were not successful. Even as we talked we both heard the distinct sound of a chuckle in the corner behind Barbara's chair.

I spun to face that direction, but there was nothing -- just the silence to mock us after the uncanny sound.

We tried to settle down to the UFO problem again.

"Do you really believe that the people who built the pyramids are in the UFO game too?" she asked me.

"Yes, I do. While I was in Egypt I naturally went to see the pyramids, climbing to the top, both inside and outside. I found it all most interesting, and went to see the tombs which are down below the Sphinx. And in Cairo I came to know a young man who was a curate of the Egyptian Museum. I mentioned the Sun Stella to him----"

"What is the Sun Stella, Johnnie," Barbara interrupted.

"It's a very large slab of sandstone which rests between the paws of the Sphinx. On it can be seen many hieroglyphics, which once were translated, but I cannot remember now what it all meant. However, I mentioned the Sun Stella to my good friend, and he nodded.

"'Yes, John, it is a genuine treasure. From it we have found much to explain the life of a past race. Of course you will know it conceals a door.'

"'A door? Where does it go to, George?'

G. DUPLANTIER

"'It conceals a door which gives access to a rather long passage beneath the Sphinx, which in turn leads to a secret chamber beneath the pyramid of Cheops.'"

I explained to Barbara that Cheops was the largest of the three pyramids.

"I asked George what this secret chamber was used for. He replied, 'It is not used these days, John. But it was used in a far away age when Amenhotep was Pharaoh. And beyond the wall of that chamber is yet another smaller one. And it is in that smaller chamber we find the secret of the earth's future.'"

"And what did he mean by the secret to our future, Johnnie?" asked Barbara.

"I asked him that, too, but he wouldn't tell me any more, although I felt, and still feel, that he knew a lot more than he told me.

"And what would you say was in that smaller chamber?"

"I don't know, Barb. But I have an idea, though, and it is one which I wouldn't be game to speak of. It's too startling and fantastic," I told her quietly.

"Wouldn't you tell ME?" she inquired.

"Yes, one day soon I'll tell you."

The following days brought us many new reports, and among them were two from the South Island; but these were undoubtedly meteors. But the reports on them in the press proved just how simple it is to be confused with meteors and UFOs.

Some of the descriptions: "A large object resembling an orange tennis ball; A bright wriggly thing with a trail of smoke stretched out behind a flying saucer; A weird ball of fire shooting sparks every where; A flaming mass shooting through the sky."

This, we admitted, was a case for the scoffers, and we knew how they would laugh their empty heads off, knowing too that these people would forget that the serious researcher had already dismissed the report as nothing more startling than a meteor.

"What would be the explanation of the scoffers regarding the objects seen at the Nato exercise?" I mused.

"Balloons," grinned Barbara.

"And how about this one? 'Strange Object Seen In Sky

From City and Huntly.' Five people saw this, and it sounds like quite a good report. I suppose it was a balloon, though. Or it could be a piece of meteoric rock as was once claimed by our local astronomer, Mr. Bryce, eh?"

"What else is there, Johnnie?" laughed Barbara.

"This one says that a strange object fell from the sky after three mysterious explosions. Wonder what it was?"

"That was Venus, Jonnnie, only the planet was having a bit of trouble," she laughingly remarked.

That was June, 1954. A beautiful evening. Clear and rather mild. The terror was closer to us now, and soon the pressur would increase to force out of this research. But on this evening there was nothing to fear and we walked in the moonlight, still discussing the theory we had thought out. We strolled along, lost in the world of mystery, and I was rather startled when Barbara suddenly came up with:

"Do you really and honestly believe I am in danger from these things, Johnnie?"

"Yes," I answered grimly. "I do."

"And what are they likely to do to me?" she enquired, adding one terrible possibility.

I stopped and gripped her shoulders, staring down at her. "That could happen too!" I said harshly. "Doesn't that scare you?"

"I don't know, Johnnie," she replied. "I suppose that if it did happen I'd be terrified. But the thought doesn't worry me very much." She grinned at my serious expression. "Anyway, nothing has happened to me yet, so why worry?"

"'Nothing has happened yet!'" I echoed. "Can't you realize what could happen to you?"

"Yes, I do, Johnnie. And I refuse to be frightened!" she replied with some spirit. Then she said, rather strangely, "But I might like to meet a space man. I wonder what one'd be like?"

"Stop it!"

"I think I'd kiss him, y'know," she said with a grin.

"You might get one heck of a shock if you did see one of these things!"

"Something like a satyr?"

"Yes."

"The satyr and the nymph. Me, of course, being the nymph?"

"Barbara, I can't understand your silly talk about this! You don't seem particularly concerned about it all, do you?"

"No. Why should I? I haven't been hurt yet, as I have already said, and should they attack me, well, that is when the time will come to worry."

Her attitude rather frightened me, and that evening when I said good night to her I again warned her to take care.

"Look, Johnnie. I'm all right. Now stop being a silly goat! I'm not going to be harmed!" She was soon lost in the darkness as she moved away.

CHAPTER TWELVE
I SEE THE DISC

I stood there, pondering her strange attitude, and wondered if she were as relaxed as she made herself appear to be. I didn't like it at all. The fear was growing in me that they would strike at her. Would I be able to protect her? What would happen? When would it happen? I began to feel that the attack was coming, and beads of perspiration formed on my forehead as I thought of Barbara being used as a plaything of some heinous thing. I was trembling. With a cigarette lit I felt a little better, and my wife, just arriving from her lodge meeting brought a happy smile on my face.

"Hullo, you're out late, boy."

"Yes. I was just thinking of the UFOs, darling. I don't know if we're making any progress, but it could be that we have stumbled on something pretty big. Dunno yet." I threw my cigarette away and lit another, and the action did not escape my wife's attention.

"What are you worried about, John?"

"Nothing, dear," I lied. "Just tired, that's all. I drew on my cigarette, and, looking up at the stars, remarked, "It's just the sort of evening to see a saucer. Y'know, darling, that's what I'd like to do."

"You've seen them before."

"I know. But I'd like to have a fair dinkum close look at one. Be rather interesting, wouldn't it?"

"For you and Barbara it would be very interesting. But I'm going to bed. Coming in?"

"Shortly, darling. I'll finish my cigarette before I do. Anyway, I may see a saucer."

I leaned against the gate staring upward, still thinking of Barbara's strange manner. I tried to force it from me, but the feeling persisted in my mind. She was in danger. But how to make her realize it? I wasn't going to accept her claim that there was no fear in her mind that she would be attacked; but if such an attack did take place, what would happen. What force would be used? And what form would an attack take? Would it affect her sanity? Would she still be able to carry on our research? A thousand similar questions raced through my mind.

Did she really have fears that an attack would take the form she suggested? It was almost too frightening to think about! But the fact remained that she thought they would attack her in such fashion. What if this should come about when I wasn't present? How could I protect her then?

My thoughts were interrupted by a light. I straightened up. It was very high and moving slowly. North to south. It must be all of 10,000 feet, I thought. It was now at an angle of about 70 degrees to my eyes. Quite big, really. Not a meteor -- not moving fast enough. It stopped, as I watched with some excitement.

Now it was growing bigger and had changed from a reddish-orange to a duller yellow. Still very bright, though. Still bigger. I could now make out its shape. Bell-like. Still a dullish yellow. It was now down to about 200 fett! And still descending.

It descended to about 100 feet above me, or maybe a littl higher . I stared at it. It was rocking slightly. I estimated it was about 30 feet across, and maybe slightly higher from rim to the round ring I could see on top. Up near the top of the objec was a row of circular portholes, and from these a bright light shone. It was pulsating a little, while a band, containing the ports, revolved slowly. Underneath I was able to make out three ball things, which I decided could be its landing gear. At the height where it was I decided it was a dark grey in color, although it was hard to be definite. I detected no sound from the object, but after it had hung there for about ten minutes (this again is difficult to be certain of, owing to the excitement I felt), it suddenly rose to a great height and raced away to the south.

I stood there, trying to collect my excited thoughts, and made myself realize that I had seen a UFO at very close quarters. I was sorry that my wife hadn't hear me call to her.

I hurried inside to tell my wife of what I had just seen, and my excitement was sufficient to prove to her that there certainly had been something there. I was very keen to find a witness, and discovered that there was one! I was safe now from ridicule.

The next night I related the details of the sighting to Barbara, and she questioned me closely. She was most convinced that I had actually seen it. We then returned to our Antarctica theory, and this in turn brought us back to Bender's affair, and after discussing our previous view, we turned to Edward Jarrold of Australia.

"Who was Ed's visitor," she asked.

"He might have been from Australian Air Force Intelligence," I replied. "He did tell us in his letter that he was onto something pretty big, and that he had been invited to meet a bloke from R.A.A.F. Intelligence. And you remember we have his report on the meeting. No, I don't believe it was an official from Air Force, Barb."

"H'm. Well, who the blue blazes was the bloke?" she asked impatiently.

"Haven't a clue on that one, I'm afraid."

"Harold Fulton might know, mightn't he?"

"Granted. But we can't ring Harold up and say, 'Look, Harold, old boy, who was Ed's visitor?' Can we?"

"Oh I know that, you idiot."

"Well, what can we do?"

Barbara shook her head. "Oh, I suppose we will have to leave it for the moment, eh? Let's have another look at this area...." She stopped suddenly to look across the room with a strained expression. A frown crossed her face, and then her eyes turned to mine.

I had also heard it. A kind of whosper. I felt that it came from somebody who had been listening to our conversation, and had whispered some comment to it! I was ready to face anything I could see, but when it came to something invisible, I didn't feel so confident! I tensed as Barbara held my arm in her hand, her startled whisper breaking the tension.

"What....was it, Johnnie?"

I sensed the fear she felt, and to calm her nerves, I tried to laugh, failing miserably. "Oh....I reckon we were just hearing things, my dear."

Her eyes roved the room, and she asked grimly, "Were we?" Her hand was shaking as she held out her cigarettes. I took one and flicked my Ronson. "I'm frightened, Johnnie!"

"But I'll look after you, Barbara, I said, hoping my words would calm her.

"I....I....let me sit near you." She moved her chair next to mine and I put my arms around her waist, feeling her trembling body. Did we hear the sound, or was it just a case of hearing things? Had just one heard the whisper, it would be different, but we had both heard it. "What is it, John?" she asked fearfully. Have we discovered something? Something we aren't supposed to know? Is that it?" she asked me, her eyes demanding an answer.

"Yes," I admitted wearily, "I do believe we know more than is safe for us."

CHAPTER THIRTEEN
THE HIDEOUS THING

"Look, Barbara, you've got to get out before it's too late!" I warned. "It's you they'll hurt. You're a girl!

"I refuse to give up!" she told me firmly, and again her eyes widened. Her slim body stiffened. "What....what was that?" she whispered.

A distinct sound of breathing came from across the room! And it sounded as if the breather had a serious case of asthma. Then it stopped, and I nervously lit a cigerette, not knowing quite how to tackle a problem such as this. I didn't try, for I realized I was doomed to failure before I even started. But my companion was afraid now, and her earlier words were forgotten. It was quite early when I said goodnight to her at the gate, my mind filled with thoughts of danger for her. This fear was to grow in intensity as the days went by, and would continue until the first of the horrifying attacks, only then to become greater!

What was to be next? Had we known, F.S.I. would have closed down there and then, forgetting that there were UFOs to be studied. But we didn't know. So far the attacks, if they were caused by our research, had not been too serious. They had shaken us considerably, a lot more than I was prepared to admit. I was almost at the stage where I was looking over my shoulder at each step. My health began to suffer. Barbara looked wan and tired, and I knew she was afraid, too. But we persisted in our research, and soon were to be sorry that we had not heeded the warnings. The terror was about to strike!

That Friday evening was much the same as any other, though I later felt most thankful that my wife had been out with a girl friend. Barbara and I settled down to talk; then soon afterward she realized she was out of cigarettes and decided to go to the store after a pack.

I got myself a pot of beer, and sat down with it. The "sounds" still concerned me. I glanced at my watch. Ten minutes. I continued to think. Another look. Twenty minutes had passed, and still there was no sign of Barbara. I became anxious about her safety. Another look at my watch, and still another. By then I was very anxious. I got up and started to walk back and forth across the lounge. Suddenly the front door flew open, and a figure rushed into my arms. Barbara said in a voice filled with fear, "There's something out there!"

Quickly releasing her, I hurried outside, stopping on the top step as a terrible stench struck me. I almost fainted in terror. It was like burnt plastic and sulphur. I stood there for a moment, and then walked down to the front gate, neither seeing nor hearing anything. I retraced my steps, seeing Barbara was on the upper step, watching me. I searched the rear of the grounds, finding nothing, and had just started to return to the door when I heard distinct sounds behind me. I stopped and shone my torch. There was nothing there. I walked on. The sounds followed. I stopped and the sound stopped. I moved. It moved. Again I stopped, was amazed and startled when "it" kept on! The peculiar shuffling, scraping sound went past me, and I felt something solid brush against my shoulder! This was the first indication I'd had that "they" were solid as I!

As the sound continued toward the front gate, I slowly walked to the door, joining Barbara. I asked her if she had heard it.

"Yes, Johnnie. It was the same as I heard outside when I came from getting the cigarettes. I saw fear living in her eyes, and I wanted to send her away. But now it was too late. I poured two brandies, and told her I was going out for another look around.

"I'm coming, too, Johnnie," she told me firmly.

I shook my head. "You're going to stay here!"

She came closer, and tried to smile. "But, if I'm with you, Johnnie, I'll be safer than here on my own. Won't I?" she asked with logic.

"All right," I agreed. "Only stay close to me!"

"Yes, Johnnie," she said, a little meekly. I felt her hand on my arm as I walked along the path to the rear of the house. I turned the corner, stopping in horror, feeling, more than seeing, Barbara move to my side.

We stared at the evil thing which faced us about 27 feet

G. DUPLANTIER

across the lawn. It was loathsome. Hideous. Evil. Disgusting. Horrifying.

It was about eight feet in height. I don't profess to be a hero, nor am I a coward, but this thing was sufficient to cause me a lot of natural fear. We stood transfixed, staring in complete horror at the monster in the exceptionally bright moonlight. I felt a desire to take Barbara and run as fast as possible from it, but I discovered I had no will-power to move a finger. I was helpless!

I forced myself to pay some attention to its appearance, wanting to hold my companion close in protection, for even at that moment I had some premonition of what was to come.

The monster's head was large and bulbous. No neck. A huge and ungainly body supported on ridiculously short legs. It had webbed feet. The arms were thin and not unlike stalks of bamboo. It had no hands, the long fingers jutting from the arms like stalks. Its eyes were about four inches across, red in color. There was no nose, just two holes, and the mouth was simply a straight slash across its appallingly lecherous face. The whole was a green lime in color, and it was possible to see red veins running through its ungainly form. The monster was definitely male.

Barbara's eyes opened wide in fear and shocking horror at the sight of this monster. She was not moving in any way, and I felt she was held powerless as was I. We were at the mercy of the odiously base thing.

I almost wept with distracted terror as I understood the intentions of the hideous thing. I strove frantically to move, inwardly moaning that I was held in the power of the terror before us. It was now moving toward us, its filthy eyes fixed on Barbara's slim body. I shuddered. Completely frantic now, I tried to pray, but the words just wouldn't form in my mind. Still closer, its spindly arms lifted toward her body. I felt the sweat trickle down my face, my chest and my back. The fingers were now almost touching her shirt.

I tried to yell her name as Barbara seemed to come into complete mental control of the monster, and I will spare the reader Barbara's actions. This wasn't my little friend! She was a stranger! She had to be! She seemed to be waiting for the filthy hands to touch her!

The arms lifted more and only a hair's breadth now separated her body from its fingers. I saw all this in the moonlight as I watched helplessly, knowing I couldn't stop it carrying out its hideous attack. I could only watch in terror.

It was our master and it was making Barbara obey its instructions. It was the only answer! It had to be the answer.

But just at what seemed to be the critical moment, the thing withdrew its hands from her and moved slowly back to where it had been standing when we first saw it. Then it disappeared from sight.

Barbara moaned and fell into my arms, and she shook uncontrollably. I got her into the lounge, eased her into a chair and got her some brandy. Her lips were moving, but there was no sound. I knelt in front of her, holding her hands, feeling with my free one for some cigarettes.

"What....what was it, Johnnie?" she whispered in terror.

"God above knows, dear! I don't!"

She nodded slowly, and then said in a strained voice, "You saw...what it made me do?" Tears overflowed now, and her young body shook.

"Yes," I told her miserably, "I know."

"I'll be all right, Johnnie," she whispered. "I got a fright, that's all."

"I'll take you home, Barbara."

She nodded. "Home. Home to what, Johnnie?"

She smiled grimly. "Home to another attack? Maybe it will come back. Yes," she continued as if in a daze, "it might come back again. This time I won't escape from it." Her words stopped as she saw the expression of terrible fear in my eyes.

"Please, Johnnie," she whispered. "Nothing is going to happen. It won't come back. Take me home," she asked.

"I'm not leaving you alone!"

"You certainly can't spend the night in my room," she grinned bravely. "Look, Johnnie, I'll be safe. Dinkum, I will."

"All right. Come on." I walked along with her, amazed at her efforts to sound quite normal as she chattered to me. It was an act. But a very brave one. She swung her hand as it gripped mine, and said brightly, "I'd like to kiss you, Johnnie. Shall I?"

"Would that make you feel any better?"

"Very much better," and she pulled my head down and kissed me on the cheek warmly.

At the house I had to leave her alone, but the rest of the night was long, and sleep was far away from me; I was too afraid that the telephone would ring and I wouldn't hear it. At last, though, dawn broke and the birds sang as I told my wife of the shocking attack. After breakfast I sat in my chair, my thoughts chaotic and grim, and later I sat on the front step. Questions tumbled through my mind with a speed that left me breathless. What was it? Where did it come from. Why did it attack us? What was behind it? Would it return? Was Barbara safe from another attack? How could I protect her? I lit another cigarette and walked to the corner, staring across the lawn to where it had stood, almost again seeing it, in my mind's eye. I shuddered and returned to the steps, still deep in thought. I jumped as a voice greeted me, and I looked up at the strangely beautiful girl who faced me, a look of curiosity in her lovely eyes.

"Hullo, Terry," I smiled and rose to my feet.

"You're very grave this morning, John," she said in her lilting voice, and sat on the step. "I....I would like to talk to you. Do you mind?"

"I feel deeply honored that you have joined me, fair lady," I murmured sincerely.

She appeared nervous, and at last said, hesitantly, "John ...Would....oh! Listen, did you see anything on your back lawn last evening?" she hurriedly asked.

I stiffened and lit a cigarette, lifting my head in surprise. "What was there?" I asked tensely.

She drew a small pad from her pocket and quickly sketched. She handed it to me. "This!"

I stared at the very same "green thing" Barbara and I had seen. Terry had drawn a remarkable likeness, almost as hideous as the actual thing. Hardly a detail was missing, and I knew she had seen the same thing.

"We both saw it, Terry. It...it was absolutely hideous," I said, forcing the words from my tight throat. I told her what had occurred, right from the start, and found it made me feel much better.

"It was going to....do something awful to Barbara," she

gasped in horror, her slim hand on my arm.

"Yes, Terry. That is about what it was going to do when whatever controlled it, and God knows what that was, called it back from her. I was in a terrible fever the whole time, and did everything I knew how to break the power it held me under. I had to stand there and watch it all." I felt ill at the memory.

"Where were you?"

"Just around the corner, Terry. That's why you couldn't see us, although you could see the monster on the lawn."

"It didn't hurt Barbara?" Terry asked in sincere concern.

"She was terribly afraid after it was over, but there was no physical harm," I told her. Then I added, "Fortunately!"

"Yes, fortunately," she said softly. Soon after that she left me, and I watched as she walked quietly along the path. I returned to my thoughts and soon saw Barbara smiling down at me.

CHAPTER FOURTEEN
THE CREATURE RETURNS

"Hullo, Johnnie. You look all in," Barbara greeted me.

"You are the one who should be ill, Barbara, but I feel terrible."

"You look it, too, John! Did you tell your wife?"

"Yes. I told her as I lay in bed at dawn. It was so strange to be telling her of the terror while outside the birds sang happily. Nothing further happened to you? No troubles?"

"None, Johnnie," she told me."I took some aspirins and went to bed. I slept right through the night. She didn't tell me that she had taken so many tablets that she had put herself into a drugged sleep. I did not learn that until much later.

"Terry came over to see me this morning. She saw the thing too."

Barbara gasped. "She...saw it too?" Her eyes were wide. "But...if she saw the thing, she must have seen everything!"

"No, she wasn't able to see us. Just the thing."

"Strike! What a shock for little, sweet Terry."

I nodded. "Yes, it was a shock, but it didn't stop her from making a sketch of it. Every detail was there, and it proved that she saw it."

"Strewth!" was Barbara's reply. "What a girl!"

We talked about the thing because it had to be discussed.

We had to talk about it to find some answer, to find some defense against another similar episode.

"Well, as Terry saw the thing, it proves it was there, doesn't it? It was fair dinkum, alright," nodded my companion.

"Of course it was fair dinkum! It wasn't a nightmare we had last night, girl!" I almost yelled at her. "And, my dear, you're going to pull out before it's too late!"

Her head turned, and she stared at me in amazement. "I'm going to...what?" she gasped. "Look, if you think I'm going to be scared out of this business, you've got to think again! I'm in this, and in it I'm going to stay!" She lit herself a fresh cigarette. "Pull out! Just because that ugly thing appeared and did what it did! It's not enough to frighten me out of all this! I'm not a coward!" She almost shouted.

"I didn't say you were a coward! But I'm not going to stand by and see the same thing happen again!"

She looked down at her cigarette. "I'm sorry, Johnnie! You couldn't have helped me, even though you had tried." This was in answer to the inference that I stood by and couldn't help her.

I knew we hadn't seen the last of this thing, and I knew somehow that she would be in danger again. I was terribly afraid for her safety, but deeply shocked as I saw again and again that I would be powerless to save her. Whatever we might have dreamed regarding the next attack, it was ought to have been what actually happened! It was one affair I will always remember for its ferocity, and for the harm they did to my young friend. I know that somewhere in our research we stumbled onto the truth, and they were determined to frighten us sufficiently so that we would be silent. I pointed this out to Barbara a number of times over the following evenings, but she was adamant that we were going to carry out our efforts. As she gradually recovered from her terrible fright, we found we could discuss the attack with a calm outlook -- but we never did arrive at any particular answers.

Then, one evening, just before the end came, I again escorted Barbara home, amused at her chatter of happiness. There was nothing in the air to show us there was anything to fear, and she even facetiously remarked that one evening perhaps she would meet a space man in her room. I told her not to talk like that, but she only laughed delightedly. At her door, however, it was different, and she asked me to search the room for her. I found nothing, and it wasn't until the following day that I remembered the very slight, but most peculiar odor I had detected. There had been the usual feminine odor of powders, perfumes and the usual makeup, and these registered in my mind. But there had also been the other smell, like burned plastic or sulphur. My overlooking this was a terrible mistake, for it was that night when they struck again. And they struck while she was alone!

I left her and walked home, unaware as I lay in bed reading that she was undergoing a terror such as a human had never known! And it was not until many hours later that I learned of the hideous attack they launched upon this defenseless girl; when I did learn about it I marvelled at the manner in which she managed to retain her sanity in spite of the horrors she had known.

I saw her the following day, and was uneasy when I detected she was walking in some sort of daze -- or a horror-filled dream. And that evening she told me all that had befallen her after I left her alone. I saw the vile scene as she spoke! A terrible coldness gripped my stomach, and I wondered how any girl could have endured such horror and remained sane! She sat at my side, her hand resting on mine, and there was a slight trembling, but her voice was surprisingly calm. She seemed to be quite unmoved, but I was aware that she was on the verge of hysterical tears. After she had related the ghastly details of the attack, she typed a report on it in ghastly completeness. I read it. It was all there. A shocking testimony of fear!

I will abridge this report in presenting it to the reader, for only a few could peruse it without becoming ill -- if it were presented as Barbara wrote it:

"When I entered my room last evening I immediately noticed a peculiar odor, but decided it came from outside. Also I did not want to mention this to Johnnie for fear it would unduly alarm him. I undressed and drew on my dressing gown, planning to have a bath before retiring. On my return from bathing, I removed my gown and sat down on my bed to smoke a cigarette. It was a very warm night.

"Suddenly I had the impression that I was not alone, that unseen eyes were studying me. This impression was so strong that I searched the room, finding nothing. I returned to sit on the bed, and to go over in my mind some of the research John and I were doing. The impression of unseen eyes persisted, but I forced myself to ignore it, preferring to think of our investigative tasks.

"I crushed my cigarette out and turned to pick up my pajamas, freezing as someone touched my shoulder. I jerked upright, my eyes closed in fear. I found that I was unable to move. I gradually mustered the will-power to force my eyes open to see my attacker, I almost fainted away! I could see nobody in the room! Whatever or whoever it was, it was invisible!

"Hours seemed to pass, during which time I seem to be able to remember all details. I tried to think of my friend, John, and his grin, but all I could think of was the horror that I was experiencing.

"Finally the horror was gone. The attack ceased as suddenly as it had begun. I dragged myself to a sitting position and stared at my body, shuddering as I saw the fine scratches I was covered with. With a trembling hand I lit a cigaretta and looked at my watched. Two and a half hours had passed! I tried to think clearly, and eventually forced my mind to accept what had happened to me. Sleep was far away and I tried to find an answer to this new development in the UFO research I had embarked upon.

"I concluded that the thing had been solid, even if invisible. There was, of course, no way of knowing exactly what it was like, and I tried to form a picture in my mind to fit it, but I gave up in fear. I got into bed and eventually fell into a deep sleep filled with nightmares. With the light of day, I again looked at my body and shuddered when I saw the scratches. It had really happened after all! I felt sick, but I knew I would have to go to work, for to remain in my room all day would drive me completely mad!"

I listened to all Barbara told me in silence, almost petrified with horror at the bestial terror she had experienced at the hands of this invisible thing. I was not particularly keen to question her, but realized it was the only way we might solve the identity of the thing. When I asked her if she felt well enough to answer some questions, she nodded.

"Yes, Johnnie, I'm ready."

"What size would you estimate the thing to have been?"

"Much taller than you. Well over six feet or more." And in reply to the texture of its skin, she replied, "It was like sandpaper. Very rough."

"Did you notice any particular odor?"

"About the same as we noticed the evening we saw the green thing. A little."

"Would you say it was anything like the green thing?"

"I couldn't say. It was invisible."

"Was there any sound?"

"None. Except for my own breathing."

"Did you notice any shadows?"

"Yes, when I first opened my eyes I saw a faint shadow against the wall at the head of my bed. It was a shadow of a man, only it was clearer below the waist."

"You had no trouble in seeing this?"

"None, because I was partly facing that way."

"You say you attempted to force it from you. Will you show me your hands? Palms up?" (I looked at her hands and saw there were fine scratches covering the skin.)

"I see." I watched as she stood up, pulling her shirt free from the waist band of her slacks. "What are you doing, Barbara?" I asked her apprehensively."

"Forgive me, John, but this is something you must see!"

She faced me, calm, unmoving, and I stared at her, appalled at the scratches which covered the most of her body. I looked at her ribs closely, noting two brown marks about the size of an American 10-cent coin. I mentioned these, and she told me, "They appeared there after the thing left, Johnnie. I don't know what caused them." She slowly dressed and sat down again, her voice now telling of the fear she felt.

"What was it, Johnnie?" She almost whispered. "Why did it do it?"

"God above knows that, my dear," I replied a little lamely.

"Just one last question," I added. "You say it seemed to be only clinically interested in you, despite what it did? When did you get that impression?"

"It didn't seem to be very sensual. Just curious, that's all."

During the following weeks I saw the fight had died within her, and I knew there was little hope of our continuing this research to which we had dedicated ourselves. The months had taken their toll of me, too, and the fears I had known, the strain of too little sleep, had combined to undermine my health.

I realized the time had come to rest completely. Only after such a rest would I be able to return to my investigations with any vigor.

Barbara informed me she was returning to her home, and I encouraged this, for to have made her change her mind could have been fatal to her. I felt lost without her to talk to, but I told myself I would return to the research alone.

But it was not to be. "They" were to have the final word in this strange drama.

CHAPTER FIFTEEN
THE ENDING

For two days after Barbara's departure I rested, trying to forget the terrible experience she had endured, and then I felt an urge to make one further attempt to find some solution to the problem of Antarctica.

I had no kidea of just how I would know if I did find a solution, but anything would be better than doing nothing at all. I surrounded myself with papers, reports, notes, our huge map and my reference books. I worked hard, analyzing reports, studying each minutely in the hope that something would give me a new lead. But each minute brought back the vision of Barbara's scratched body, and I felt a fear grow that I was only asking for more trouble. I knew that by this diregard of the warnings I could be putting my wife in danger. I thought they would move against me first, for there was nothing my wife knew of the affair, apart from details of the attacks already made. This made me feel better, and I returned to my work.

The morning sped by. I was no further advanced. Lunch was over, and I returned to poring over the map, tensing when the doorbell rang.

It was Terry.

I sat at my desk, looking at this strangely lovely young girl. Twenty-one. Tall, for a girl. Slim, with a superb figure. Graceful as the legendary Diana. I had a deep respect for her, and usually felt that I was in the presence of a young Greek Goddess when she called to talk. I studied her as she relaxed in a deep chair, her soft hair forming a halo for her lovely face.

"It's nice of you to call, Terry," I said quietly. "May

I get you a drink?"

"Thank you, John," she murmured, her blue eyes smiling with some inner amusement. She carefully lit one of her cigarettes with real rose petal tips and glanced at the huge map. "What are all those lines, for?" she asked.

I explained the map, told her briefly of what we had been working on before our troubles.

"Will Barbara be joining you today?"

"Barbara's gone home," I replied. "She had a terrible experience a few weeks ago, and it was too much for her. She thr it in." I was afraid she would question me about what had happen and I lit another cigarette to cover my nervousness.

"What happened, John?"

"Believe me, Terry, when I say it was a shocking matte that is about all I can tell you!"

"Why? I'm broadminded, John."

"It's all in a report she wrote up, but I'm afraid it would shock and frighten you."

"Why does everyone treat me like a child?" she exclaim petulantly. "You treat me as if I were some goddess out of a pag in Greek mythology, John!"

I took Barbara's report from the pile of papers at my side, nervously handed it to her and watched her start to read. As she read her brow first wrinkled, and then I could see shocked amazement in her eyes. She completed it and looked up.

"It must have been terrible for Barbara," was her only comment.

"Yes, I saw the scratches this thing left on her, and I know Barbara told the truth."

"But why didn't you heed the warnings you had been given. You should have known better than to pursue this matter so far!"

"Maybe I didn't take them seriously."

"And the result was that....." She paused.... "We have this report. And yet, in spite of that, you're still working on this strange thing?"

"Yes."

"Have you ever thought that you might be fighting against the forces of Satan?" This question was unlike Terry. She continued, "No, I'm not a religious crank! And I am trying to be serious!"

"The idea did occur to me once, but I refused to believe it."

"And after this thing happened to Barbara at her home, you still refuse to believe it?"

"I don't know what to think, Terry."

"What about your wife? Arent't you afraid these things might attack her?" she asked quietly.

"I don't believe she knows enough to be troubled."

She smoothed her hands over her modest skirt. "In your place, John, I'd be very worried." She stood up and smiled down at me, and I rose. "You're playing with a dangerous weapon. Why not give up?" she asked very seriously.

"I will." I looked at the map. "Yes, it is a dangerous weapon to toy with, isn't it? There mightn't be any more warnings " I drew on my cigarette. "Why the bloody hell didn't she listen to me? I told her to give up! But she refused to stop! And the result was......." I stopped because I didn't want to think about it.

After she had left, I returned to my research and the hours fled by. I emptied my ashtray many times. I looked at my watch. 1:30 A.M. Time to stop. Time to go to bed. It sounded good to get some rest. I looked up quickly. Tense. Nervous. That sound!

I rose and decided to look outside. I heard it again. I didn't like it. It came again. A sound too hard to describe. One which made my hair almost stand on end. I wiped my brow. The room was turning cold on this summer night, or I was in a cold sweat. I knew there was some evil force present and I felt fear go down my spine. I looked about me.

And then I saw "it"!

The thing was about four or five feet away from me. It

was facing me in all its vile, base hideousness. Its body resembled, vaguely, that of a human. From the waist up it was a man, and from the waist down that of a woman. Its flesh, stinkingly putrid, seemed to hang in folds. It was a greyish color. Evil exuded from the entire thing. The slack mouth was dribbling, and the horrible lips began to move, but there was no sound.

I realized with a shock that it was talking to me, using telepathy to converse. I was being warned not to proceed any further with my research. It seemed to laugh at me, and told of how others had suffered because they had attempted to solve the enigma. Like Barbara!

It told me, "Your friend knew too much and had to be silenced. We sent one of us to her as a warning. We weren't ready to allow it to complete its task at that time...."

The thing told me in obscene words what Barbara had experienced, and each word was accompanied with what seemed to be laughter. I abridge this "conversation" somewhat in the telling of it here.

I asked, mentally, "How many were present?"

"Thirteen of us. Only three were actually involved."

"Why did you scratch her?"

"It was something we couldn't avoid."

"Where did the two brown marks come from?"

"They are there to remind her of us," the thing again told me by telepathy.

At that point the thing seemed to waver, and grow less distinct; then materialized again into solidity. I almost collapsed in horror and revulsion as the male and female areas of its body had suddenly changed places.

"You have been warned! Take heed! Should you fail there will be others to suffer!" Slowly it moved closer. "You have told another of your research. Tell her no more! Or we will have our revenge upon her! You understand?" The thing gloated, its slack mouth dribbling sickeningly.

"Terry!" I cried out.

"That is what we know you to call her. She too will

suffer if you are foolish!"

"Why harm her?" I asked harshly. "She has nothing to do with my research!"

"Already she knows what you have told her!" It lifted its hands a little. "If you persist, you will soon see what we can do!"

Its foul eyes were now like chips of granite. Shortly it began to waver; then it just dissolved and was gone.

It had warned me to leave alone.....or else! I now saw fully the dangers I was against and broke into a cold sweat. Why had they now selected Terry as their victim? I felt thankful that they had not threatened my wife. She knew as much as I. Was it because of the gold cross she wore around her neck? Might that not be a protection.

But the danger clearly wasn't worth it, and I knew the end of my research had indeed arrived. I would have to quit. I would go away on a holiday.

I went away to Auckland and stayed with my old mother, resting my nerves, trying to bring my shocked system back into order. The strain of the days behind weighed heavily upon me. As I lay in the sun, trying to forget, the vision of the green thing returned to taunt me, and again I could visualize the scratches on poor Barbara's body. And there was nobody to tell of the experiences, so it would remain locked away in my tortured mind. I couldn't even write and tell Gray Barker.

I wondered what he would say if I sent a letter relating the final happenings. No, it couldn't be done. But he had to be warned of the danger behind this research. I did finally decide to write him, but to alter the circumstances and still warn him.

I want it known that ever since that day I have regretted this evasion. Gray had always been a sincere friend, and I should have realized at the time that he would have accepted that which was really the truth.

I do not yet fully understand the strange circumstances and phenomena which I ran against in the course of my research, and, when I wonder about this, and realize that I deliberately gave an altered version of what actually happened both to Gray Barker and to Harold Fulton, I also wonder about other researchers and if the information they have given out to explain their "hush-ups" could have been, through reason of their best judgments, also altered somewhat.

I think that this unpleasant and frightening account should be ended as soon as possible, so I will be brief:

Two years later I returned home and heard the malicious lies which had been spread regarding me. One of the lies claimed I had "gone away with the girl," and there were other stupidities.

I did turn back to my research, but my heart wasn't with it. I wasn't able to overlook the previous warnings. I knew my wife was too important to me to take any further risks; she was more to me than solving the enigma of the "flying saucers."

And with that thought in mind, I quietly got down my research notebooks, and on the covers of each, below the name of the organization I added a notation:

"CLOSED"

OTHER BOOKS AVAILABLE FROM SAUCERIAN PUBLICATIONS

ADAMSKI, George: COSMIC PHILOSOPHY (Privately printed book a available to serious students of Adamski's teachings, $7.00; FLYING SAUCERS HAVE LANDED, $3.50; INSIDE THE SPACE SHIPS, $3.95; Adamski's QUESTION AND ANSWERS (Booklet No. 2), 50¢

BARKER, Gray: THEY KNEW TOO MUCH ABOUT FLYING SAUCERS (Autographed on request), $3.50; THE SAUCERIAN REVIEW (100-page Review of 1955 Saucerevents), $1.50; Rare Back Issues of THE SAUCERIAN BULLETIN, 35¢ each.

BENDER, Albert K.: FLYING SAUCERS AND THE THREE MEN, $3.95; Complete bound file (offset reproduction) of SPACE REVIEW, $1.50.

BLAVATSKY, H. P.: THE SECRET DOCTRINE (2 Vol.), $7.50; ISIS UNVEILED (2 Vol.), $7.50; KEY TO THEOSOPHY, $3.50; STUDIES IN OCCULTISM, $2.50; VOICE OF THE SILENCE, $1.50.

BRANDON, Wilfred: (Brandon is a noted teacher on the etheric plane. These books dictated through the famous medium, Edith Ellis) OPEN THE DOOR, $3.00; LOVE IN THE AFTERLIFE, $3.00; INCARNATION, $3.00; WE KNEW THESE MEN, $3.00.

BROTHER PHILIP: BROTHERHOOD OF THE SEVEN RAYS (SECRET OF THE ANDES, $3.95.

CAYCE, Edgar: (Books about & Readings of) THE GREAT PYRAMID, $1.00; GOD'S OTHER DOOR, $1.00; LOST ATLANTIS, $1.50; ONE HUNDRED QUESTIONS AND ANSWERS, $1.00; MANY MANSIONS by Gina Cerminara (Based on life readings by Cayce), $4.00; THERE IS A RIVER (Story of Edgar Cayce), by Thomas Sugrue, $5.00.

DAVID-NEEL, Alexandra: MAGIC AND MYSTERY IN TIBET, $6.00; INITIATIONS AND INITIATES IN TIBET, $5.00.

DAY, Harvey: THE STUDY AND PRACTICE OF YOGA, $3.75.

FATE MAGAZINE: Most any issue 1953 onward, 35¢ each.

GRANT, Rev. W. V.: MEN IN THE FLYING SAUCERS IDENTIFIED, 50¢; MEN FROM THE MOON IN AMERICA, 50¢; THE GREAT DICTATOR WHOSE NUMBER IS 666, 50¢.

HOWARD, Dana: EARTHBORN VENUSIAN, $4.00; DIANE, SHE CAME FROM VENUS, $3.00; UP RAINBOW HILL, $4.50; KEYS TO THE CITADEL OF SPACE, $3.95; THE KINGDOM OF SPACE, $2.00.

KEYHOE: THE FLYING SAUCER CONSPIRACY, $3.95; FLYING SAUCERS FROM OUTER SPACE, $3.95; FLYING SAUCERS: TOP SECRET, $3.95.

KRASPECON, Dino: MY CONTACT WITH FLYING SAUCERS, $3.95.

MENGER, Howard: FROM OUTER SPACE TO YOU, $4.50; MUSIC FROM ANOTHER PLANET (33 1/3 LP Record), $4.95.

MICHAEL X BOOKS: The following at $2.00 each: "SECRETS OF HIGHER CONTACT" (Who are the Space People?); "THE D-DAY SEERS SPEAK" (A picture of things to come -- in startling Focus); "RAINBOW CITY AND THE INNER EARTH PEOPLF";"FLYING SAUCER REVELATIONS" (Visitors from Venus and other planets); "THE SPACEMASTERS SPEAK" (Messages from Space People to People of Earth); "RELEASE YOUR COSMIC POWERS" (Reveals the Cosmic Balance Secret); "YOUR PART IN THE GREAT PLAN" (This book

(Continued Reverse Side)

gives important Techniques); "IS HITLER ALIVE--WE WANT YOU)" (The astonishing escape of Adolph Hitler); "THE WORLD SECRET OF FATIMA" (What is the earth-shaking secret hidden until now?) "THE SEVEN GOLDEN PROPHECIES" (As revealed by the Magi, Enoch, Elder Edda, Merlin). The following at $5.00 each: "VENUSIAN HEALTH MAGIC," "VENUSIAN SECRET SCIENCE." (All Michael X Books stiff paper bound)

MICHELET, Jules: SATANISM AND WITCHCRAFT, $3.00 (Soft Bound)

OAHSPE: $10.00.

PHYLOS: A DWELLER ON TWO PLANETS, $7.50.

RAMPA, T. Lobsang: DOCTOR FROM LHASA, $4.50.

NOSTRADAMUS: THE COMPLETE PROPHECIES OF NOSTRADAMUS, $5.00.

SHAVER MYSTERY: Subscription to series of quarterly books titled "HIDDEN WORLDS" $6.00 per year, Sample, $1.50.

SHERMAN, Harold: HOW TO USE THE POWER OF PRAYER, $3.95; KNOW YOUR OWN MIND, $3.95.

STRANGES, Frank E.: FLYING SAUCERAMA (Contains many photos)$3.00

SUMMERS, Montague: HISTORY OF WITCHCRAFT, $5.00; GEOGRAPHY OF WITCHCRAFT, $10.00.

TRENCH, Brinsley Le Poer: THE SKY PEOPLE, $4.50.

Write us for Flying Saucer or Occult Titles not listed

****

OTHER BOOKS IN THIS SERIES SIMILAR TO ONE CONTAINING THIS LIST. All Stiff Bound, 60-100 Pages.

"THE BENDER MYSTERY CONFIRMED" Readers of Bender's Works Comment With their Own Ideas and Experiences. 100 PP $3.00.

"UFO WARNING" By John Stuart. Researcher Meets with startling and terrifying results. 80 PP $3.00.

"THE FLYING SAUCERS" By Rolf Telano, Tk. Com. Startling Communications from Space Explaining Saucer Sightings. 45 PP $2.00

"FLYING SAUCERS AND THE FATHER'S PLAN" By Laura Mundo. (April '53) Mankind is Helped Back to his Original Status by Space People. $3.00

"THE STRANGE CASE OF DR. M. K. JESSUP" Edited by Gray Barker, (March, 1953). Explores the suicide of UFO author and strange communications before his death. $3.00

COMING IN THIS SERIES:

"FLYING SAUCERS IN THE BIBLE" No release date set.
"THE FLATWOODS MONSTER" Souvenir Book. No release date set.
"LIFE ON A THOUSAND WORLDS" No release date set.
"THE WORLD OF KAZIK" By Albert K. Bender. No release set.

****

Order from: SAUCERIAN BOOKS, Box 2228, Clarksburg, W. Va.

www.ingramcontent.com/pod-product-compliance
Lightning Source LLC
LaVergne TN
LVHW080925110826
845155LV00039B/214
* 9 7 8 1 9 5 5 0 8 7 2 6 1 *